INSIGHT COMPACT GUIDES

Cam...
and East Anglia

GREAT LITTLE GUIDES

Compact Guide: Cambridge and East Anglia is the ideal quick-reference guide to this historic university city and its region. It tells you everything you need to know about Cambridge itself, from colleges and parks to punting and pubs, before picking out the highlights of East Anglia, with the quaint wool towns of Suffolk, timeless Constable Country, two different coasts, and some of the finest country houses in Britain.

This is one of almost 100 titles in *Insight Guides'* series of pocket-sized, easy-to-use guidebooks intended for the independent-minded traveller. *Compact Guides* are in essence travel encyclopedias in miniature, designed to be comprehensive yet portable, as well as up-to-date and authoritative.

Star Attractions

An instant reference to some of Cambridge and East Anglia's top attractions to help you set your priorities.

King's College Chapel p17

Trinity College p20

Corpus Christi Old Court p26

Botanic Gardens p28

St John's College p29

Punting p34

Ely Cathedral p35

Lavenham p43

Constable Country p45

Norfolk Coast p55

Norwich p51

CAMBRIDGE
and East Anglia

Cambridge – Ancient City of Scholarship

Prior to its rise as a celebrated seat of learning, Cambridge was a small market town on the edge of the swampy fens. The colleges which encroached on the centre were to transform it into a university-dominated town whose intellectual and architectural heritage became the envy of the world. At the same time the pre-eminence of the university gave rise to open conflicts between town and gown which were to last for over 600 years.

Gate of Virtue at Gonville and Caius College

Today the charm and ambiance of the city lies not only in the splendour of its buildings but also in its natural surroundings and green open spaces. Famous colleges such as King's, Queens', Trinity and St John's are enhanced by their setting on 'The Backs' – the lawns, gardens and tree-lined avenues lying between the rear of the colleges and the banks of the Cam – while the Courts and gardens within the colleges provide quiet sanctuaries, seemingly far removed from the bustle of the city.

Cambridge is also a market town, a busy shopping centre and the hub of a high-tech revolution. An estimated 1,000 scientific and technological companies, many based at the Science Park or in the 'Silicon Valley' on the northern edge of the city, are now benefiting from the research and expertise of the university.

5

It is remarkable that a city of 31 colleges, ever-expanding university buildings, science parks and modern shopping precincts retains the spirit of a market town. The small centre is easily explored on foot, and the architectural glories are concentrated within the heart of the city, along a half-mile stretch of the River Cam. Many visitors see no more than facades, but the true flavour of the colleges can only really be appreciated by penetrating the inner sanctums. Despite the appearance of privacy, the majority are open to the public (the most famous charge entrance fees) and are more approachable than their battlemented gate-towers might suggest.

Trinity Street bustle and busker

The origins of the university

Cambridge is not only younger than Oxford, but owes its origins to its great rival. The 1209 riots in Oxford and consequent hanging of three students prompted a body of its scholars to settle in the distant market town of Cambridge and sow the seeds of England's second university. By 1233 a formal academic community had been established, with a chancellor at its head. Religious orders, notably the Franciscans and Carmelites, who had established themselves in the city and were admitted to degrees, had considerable influence on the development of the university.

The first college was founded in 1286 by Hugh de Balsham, the Benedictine Bishop of Ely, following his unsuccessful attempt to mingle secular scholars with the monks already established at the Hospital of St John (the site now occupied by St John's College). The medieval academic community consisted of guilds of 'masters', teaching small groups of apprentice-style students. In the early days the university was virtually penniless with no property of its own and no discipline over its young, high-spirited and frequently disorderly students.

In 1318 the academic body was declared a *studium generae,* or place of general education, entitling those with a degree (normally acquired after seven years) to teach in any Christian country. Study consisted of the *Trivium,* three years of Latin grammar, rhetoric and logic, followed by *the Quadrivium,* four years of arithmetic, geometry, astronomy and music. The early colleges were small, humble institutions and it was not until the late 13th and 14th centuries that the university received funding from wealthy benefactors – usually notable ecclesiastics or aristocrats – which enabled the colleges to expand and eventually to establish the splendid buildings we see today.

Christ's College

Town versus gown

Where Town meets Gown

No sooner had an academic community been established in the market town, than feuds arose between students and townsfolk. The disputes went on for centuries, provoked by privileges bestowed by the Crown on the university, by the political sway of university over town and the poverty resulting from the colleges' expropriation of property.

Following a riot in 1261, when houses were raided and university records burnt, 16 townspeople were hanged, whereas 28 convicted scholars were later given the king's pardon. During the Peasants' Revolt in 1381, by which time eight colleges had made their mark, townsfolk attacked Corpus Christi (the largest college property owner), sacked university buildings, burnt documents and forced the university authorities to renounce their rights and privileges. These were restored by the Crown and yet further privileges were granted, including powers to prosecute profiteers and jurisdiction over the buying and selling of bread and ale. The university's domination over the market town was firmly endorsed by the demolition of a large tract of the medieval centre for the site of King's College and its chapel in the 1440s.

King's College emblem

The spate of college construction in the 15th and 16th centuries and the steady rise in the numbers of academics arriving in Cambridge brought further unrest. It was not until 1856, when the university was forced to abrogate most of its privileges by a reforming Commission, that town and gown relations began to improve. Over the last decades the university has broadened its horizons. In 1989, for the first time, Cambridge colleges received more entrants from maintained schools than from the independent sector. All the male colleges now accept female students – Magdalene, the last male bastion, reluctantly succumbing in 1989.

The colleges today

The university has 31 colleges, all of them coeducational except Newnham, New Hall and Lucy Cavendish, which admit women only. Under the umbrella of the university, the individual colleges offer a whole way of life for the students, providing accommodation, meals, pastoral care, sporting activities, entertainment and a chapel. Colleges admit their own undergraduates and organise one-to-one or small group 'supervisions'. The majority of the teaching staff of the university are also fellows or senior members of a college. Until 1882 celibacy was a condition of all fellows with the exception of professors or fellows holding a university post. Undergraduates 'come up' to Cambridge for three to four years and, whatever their subject, study for a Bachelor of Arts degree. The honours examination is called a 'tripos', a name derived from the stool or tripod on which graduates formerly sat to deliver a satirical speech at the degree ceremony.

Graduation Day

The university, to which each college is affiliated, is a self-governing body, headed by a largely ceremonial Chancellor (currently HRH Prince Philip, the Duke of Edinburgh), the main duties being conducted by the Vice-Chancellor. The university has overall responsibility for teaching, employing professors, lecturers and administrative staff, conducting examinations and conferring degrees. At the end of June the honorary BA degrees are granted at the Senate House – a traditional and elaborate affair, involving university dignitaries in ceremonial robes and students in gowns and 'ermine' hoods.

Punting on the Cam

Location and landscape

Cambridge lies 60 miles (96km) north of London, on the edge of the large expanse of reclaimed marshland known as the Fens. The town grew up on the east bank of the River Cam, which until the 19th century was the main route for ships through the Fens to the sea. Today the river is used solely by pleasure boats and notably the traditional, flat-bottomed, pole-driven, punts, that glide along the Backs or upstream to the village of Grantchester.

Cambridge is one of the main towns of East Anglia, the most easterly region of England, bulging out between the shallow North Sea inlet of the Wash to the north and the River Stour to the south. Somewhat on a limb from the rest of Britain, and largely untouched by the Industrial

Revolution, the region has managed to preserve much of its architectural and rural heritage. Characterised by broad skies and low horizons, the landscape is flat or very gently rolling, with shallow valleys and slow-flowing rivers. Though still rural, it is no longer quite the pre-war idyll of lanes, hedgerows, and woodland. Huge tracts of heath, marsh and grassland, along with miles of hedges, have given way to prairie-style, arable farming. Efforts are now being made to preserve the rich variety of wildlife, flora and fauna, with areas of heath and marshland in Norfolk and Suffolk protected as nature reserves. Three regions, the North Norfolk Coast, Suffolk Heritage Coast and Dedham Vale, have been designated by the Countryside Commission as Areas of Outstanding Natural Beauty.

The long coastline provides the most diverse scenery, from the multicoloured cliffs of Hunstanton to the heathlands and tidal estuaries of the Suffolk shores. The wetlands along both coasts are havens for ornithologists, attracting an astonishing variety of wildlife and waders; while the beaches, despite their bracing breezes, draw substantial numbers of holidaymakers in the summer months. Centuries of storms, tides and floods have consumed large parts of the coast, and in the case of Dunwich, a whole village has been lost to the sea. Meanwhile other stretches of the coast are actually extending as the action of the sea creates long banks of sand and shingle.

The region as a whole incorporates some very distinctive areas, each one with its own history and landscape. The haunting, flat Fenland north of Cambridge is one of the richest arable areas of England. Before the 17th century when the Dutch engineer, Cornelius Vermuyden, masterminded the drainage of the fens, this area was marshland, inhabited by fishermen and wildfowlers. In the 18th century windpumps were used for drainage, followed by large steam engines in the 1820s. Today the work is done by diesel engines or electric pumps. The crowning glory of this flat and, for the most part, featureless landscape is the great Cathedral of Ely, soaring above the marshes.

In the heart of East Anglia the open heathland known as Breckland was covered in dense woodland until Neolithic man, using axes made from the flint pits at Grimes Graves (near Thetford), cleared the forest for farming. Much of the heathland was enclosed in the 18th and 19th centuries and today large areas are given over to Forestry Commission conifer plantations. The main attractions here for tourists are the woodland walks and Grimes Graves, the most important pre-historic site in East Anglia.

Northeast of Breckland, the Norfolk Broads are a network of navigable rivers and lakes, formed by the flooding of holes made by medieval peat diggers. Today the waterways are a haven for boating holidaymakers, cater-

Bracing Brancaster

8

Essex landscape near Dedham

ing for every type of craft. Although much of the plant and animal life has disappeared, many of the broads are now nature reserves, attracting a variety of wildlife.

Lavenham was built on the wool trade

Wool trade

9

Driving through the empty landscapes and sleepy villages of Suffolk and Norfolk, it is hard to believe that in medieval times this was one of the most densely populated and commercialised regions of England. The broad acres of chalk and grasslands provided ideal grazing land for sheep, giving rise, between the 13th and 17th centuries, to the era of the 'golden fleece'. Huge quantities of wool were exported and from the mid-14th century the native wool and cloth industries were boosted by the arrival of expert Flemish weavers. The most eloquent evidence of this flourishing era is the profusion of magnificent flint flushwork churches, financed by affluent cloth merchants. Norfolk and Suffolk alone have over 1,000 medieval churches, from the round-towered Saxon and Norman to the great edifices of the Gothic Perpendicular style. Also built on the back of sheep and aided by the local abundance of wood and clay were the glorious timber-framed houses which still embellish the streets of 'wool' towns such as Lavenham and Long Melford. East Anglia's textile trade began to decline in the late 16th century, with the invention of the power loom (dependent on fast running water). Loss of revenue meant no funds for new buildings or renovations, resulting in a wealth of Tudor secular architecture almost untouched by time.

Ely Cathedral

In addition to the great medieval churches, the cultural legacy of East Anglia survives in its cathedrals (Ely, Peterborough and Norwich), Norman Keeps (Norwich, Castle Rising, Castle Acre, Framlingham, Orford), the relics of medieval castles, abbeys and monasteries and – from a later era – its magnificent country mansions.

Historical Highlights

c 2,000BC Late Neolithic Age. In the Breckland area (southwest Norfolk and northwest Suffolk) woodlands are cleared for farmland. At Grimes Graves deep pits are dug to extract deposits of flint to make tools and weapons.

2,000BC onwards Bronze Age farmers settle in East Anglia. From c700 BC Iron Age settlements are established along the edge of the fenland and the valleys of the Rivers Cam and Little Ouse. Hill-fort built on the Gog Magog Hills at Wandlebury near Cambridge.

AD43 Romans conquer Britain and make Camulodunum (Colchester) their capital. The Roman Age lasts about 400 years and sees the construction of towns and ports, substantial drainage of the Fens and the clearance of forest for agriculture.

61 Boadicea of the Iceni tribe heads a revolt against Roman rule, burning down London, Colchester and St Albans.

c 70 Romans build new roads crossing Cambridge and establish a small fort on Castle Hill overlooking the River Granta (now Cam).

Early 5th century Saxon invaders from northwest Germany and Denmark settle in Cambridge on the Castle Hill site; also around the Fens and the rivers flowing to the Wash. They later make southeast Suffolk the centre of the East Anglian kingdom.

673 St Ethelreda founds a monastery at Ely. Other important religious communities are founded in East Anglia, including the Benedictine monastery at Peterborough in 655.

Early 7th century Founding of churches and monasteries throughout East Anglia as Christianity begins to spread.

Late 7th century The Venerable Bede describes Cambridge as 'a desolate little city called Grantacaestir' (the old name for the city, not to be confused with present-day Grantchester).

875 Cambridge sacked by the Danes who build a port here and establish the town as a main centre. In 878 all of East Anglia becomes part of Danelaw.

c 917 Edward the Elder, King of Wessex, retakes the region for the Saxons.

1025 St Bene't's Church, Cambridge, built by the Saxons. The town is a busy port trading with Europe via the Cam, Ouse and Wash. Norfolk and Suffolk are two of the most prosperous and densely populated counties of England.

1068 The Normans, who are rapidly dominating East Anglia, destroy 27 buildings in the Castle Hill area of Cambridge and build a castle on the site of the Roman fort. They later build an Augustinian priory near the castle (moved to Barnwell in 1112), the Church of the Holy Sepulchre (the Round Church) and the Benedictine nunnery of St Radegund.

1068–71 Ely, under Hereward the Wake, is the last centre of English resistance to the Normans who break into the cathedral in 1071.

1096 Work begins on Norwich Cathedral.

1083–1189 Present cathedral of Ely built by the Normans.

1194 Norwich, granted a charter by Richard I, becomes a city with self-governing rights.

13th century The rise of the wool trade in East Anglia. Stourbridge annual fair established in Cambridge, attracting merchants and traders from East Anglia and other parts of England. Religious orders settle in Cambridge.

1207 Cambridge receives its first charter.

1209 Birth of the university. A group of Oxford scholars move to Cambridge and establish an academic community.

1261 Cambridge townspeople riot and university records are destroyed. 16 townsmen hanged, while scholars on trial go free.

1284 Founding of Peterhouse, the first Cambridge college.

14th century The wool trade flourishes throughout East Anglia. Norwich becomes the country's main centre of worsted manufacture. In Cambridge the colleges of Michael House and King's Hall (later combined into Trinity), Clare, Pembroke, Gonville and Caius, Trinity Hall and Corpus Christi are founded.

1349 Black Death kills around two-fifths of the population in East Anglian towns.

1352 Corpus Christi College founded by the Guilds of Corpus Christi and the Blessed Virgin – the first college to be established by the townspeople.

1381 Townspeople riot and university forced to relinquish rights. The revolt is quashed and the privileges restored.

1441 Founding of King's College by Henry VI. King's College Chapel founded five years later.

1510–14 Erasmus, the great scholar and humanist, teaches at Cambridge.

1534 Founding of Cambridge University Press, the oldest printing house in the country.

1536 Cambridge threatened by the Dissolution of the Monasteries under Henry VIII. Two religious houses dissolved but colleges are saved and Henry founds Trinity in 1546.

1530s–50s
Cambridge becomes a centre of Protestantism. The 'Cambridge Martyrs', Latimer, Ridley and Cranmer are burnt at the stake in Oxford.

1616 Oliver Cromwell, born in Huntingdon near Cambridge, comes up as a student to Sidney Sussex College.

1630s Start of a major Fenland reclamation project under the Dutch engineer, Cornelius Vermuyden.

1642–5 Civil War. The Cambridge colleges support the King, the town supports Oliver Cromwell.

1669 Isaac Newton becomes Professor of Mathematics at Cambridge.

19th century Rapid growth of Cambridge University, statutes reformed and academic fields expanded.

1845 Railway stations built, connecting Cambridge and Norwich with London.

1869 Girton established as the first women's college, followed by Newnham in 1872.

1874 Founding of the Cavendish Laboratory, where research leads to the splitting of the atom in 1932.

1940s Postwar era sees the start of the transformation of rural East Anglia, by the creation of large fields through the destruction of trees and hedges and the filling in of ditches.

1947 Devastating floods in the Fens, drowning 20,000 acres of land. Lives are lost, houses ruined and sheep and cattle washed away. Further floods cause chaos in 1953.

1951 Cambridge granted city status by King George VI.

Early 1970s Cambridge Science Park established by Trinity College.

1970s Colleges start to become co-educational.

1974 County of Cambridgeshire is enlarged to encompass Huntingdonshire and Peterborough.

1983 The Kite, a former working-class quarter of Cambridge, demolished to make way for the Grafton Centre shopping complex.

1992 Historic centre of Cambridge becomes a traffic-free zone.

1994–6 Outline and master plans approved for a new satellite village for 3,000 residents near Bourn, west of Cambridge.

1997 Major deal announced in June between Cambridge University and the American software giant, Microsoft, headed by Bill Gates. Sites in west Cambridge are earmarked for a multi-million pound research centre which will be the company's first electronics research base outside the United States.

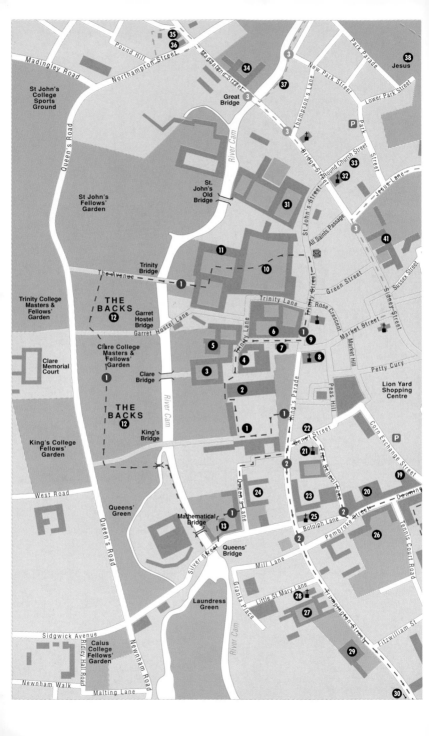

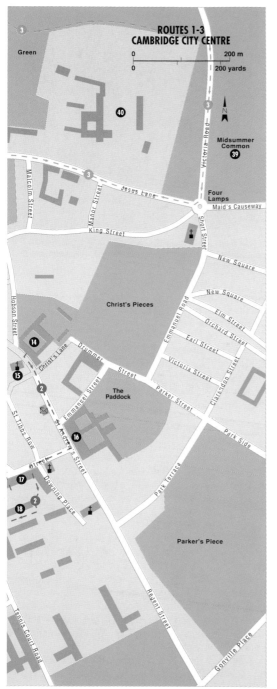

**ROUTES 1-3
CAMBRIDGE CITY CENTRE**

0   200 m
0   200 yards

*Preceding pages:
St John's New Court
and the Bridge of Sighs*

The Backs p21

15

*Pembroke College
chapel, p27*

The Quayside p32

King's College

Route 1

Colleges on the Cam

King's College and King's College Chapel – Clare – Trinity Hall – Gonville and Caius – St Mary's the Great – Trinity – The Backs – Queens' *See map, pages 14–15*

On this first route the stunning architectural ensemble of King's and the riverside colleges to the north are admired first from the city side, then from the lawns, gardens and bridges of 'The Backs'. For those who would like to try some punting, they can also be admired from the Cam.

Rose symbol of King's College

The route starts at ★★★ **King's College ❶**, whose foundation in 1441 by Henry VI involved the demolition of a large part of the medieval centre and highlighted the progressive academic control over the town. Resolute that King's College Chapel should be unrivalled in size and splendour, the King laid the foundation stone of what was to become one of the greatest late Gothic monuments in the world.

Henry VI's early plans of a college for 12 students materialised into a grandiose scheme for 70 scholars, drawn exclusively from his other foundation, Eton College. However, the royal funds for the college were continuously drawn upon for the military campaigns of the Wars of the Roses. Henry was taken prisoner in 1461 and murdered in the Tower of London ten years later. The chapel, which was the only part of King's constructed to Henry's design, took 80 years to complete.

From the King's Parade entrance to the college visitors could be forgiven for thinking that the stone screen and pinnacled gatehouse formed part of the Gothic ensemble. These were in fact added 300 years after the completion of the chapel, by the Gothic Revivalist, William Wilkins. Through the main gate, Front Court was more or less an empty space until James Gibbs built the ★ **Fellows' Building** (1724–32) on the west side (facing you). This restrained classical building was originally intended as part of a much grander scheme, to include an east and south range; but it was only in the 1820s, when Wilkins built the south range, that the Court was completed. In the centre of the square the figure on top of the fountain is the saintly Henry VI, holding 'the will and intent' – the document setting out in detail the plans for King's and Eton.

Fellows' Building

In striking contrast to Gibbs' Fellows' Building is ★★★ **King's College Chapel ➋** (usual opening hours Monday to Saturday 9.30am–4.30pm, Sunday 10am–5pm, but there are weekly variations). A late Perpendicular edifice with an interior of breathtaking beauty, this is the architectural showpiece of Cambridge. Remarkable for its sheer size, the chapel is 289ft (88.1m) long and has the largest **fan vaulted stone ceiling** in the world (80ft/24.4m high). The impression is one of magical weightlessness, the only apparent support for the vaulting (weighing around 1,875 tonnes) being the slender columns along the nave. The ornamentation on the fan vaulting, the heraldic carvings and Tudor symbolism throughout the chapel bear witness to the superb craftsmanship of the four master masons who worked on the chapel under the Tudor monarchs. Careful study reveals that, although the subjects of the motifs are repeated, each individual one differs from the next. The exquisite stained glass windows, depicting scenes from the Old and New Testaments (upper and lower levels respectively) were funded by Henry VIII. Completed in three stages, the windows change in style, the last phase showing the influence of the Italian High Renaissance in the human figures and architectural forms. The windows were the work of Flemish and English master glaziers, the majority executed between 1517 and 1547. Useful descriptions of the many different scenes are available from leaflets sold in the chapel shop.

King's College Chapel ceiling

Dividing the antechapel from the choir, the intricately carved rood screen, imitating the triumphal arches of Roman emperors, is a magnificent example of Early Renaissance woodwork. Donated by Henry VIII, its purpose was to honour the King and his new Queen, Anne Boleyn – hence the royal emblems and the carved initials of HR (Henricus Rex), RA (Regina Anna) and their entwined initials HA. The finely carved choirstalls bear the arms of Henry VI, Charles I and Eton College. From here the eye is drawn to Rubens' *Adoration of the Magi*, a masterpiece painted in 1634 for the convent of the White Nuns

Choir stalls

King's College choristers

at Louvain in Belgium and privately donated to King's in 1961. The floor of the choir, formerly raised at the east end, was levelled off to enable the painting to hang in its prominent position below the east window. A doorway from the chancel leads to the chapel exhibition, well worth visiting for displays of ecclesiastical treasures, history of the building and explanations of its construction.

Henry VI had stipulated that a choir of six men and 16 boy choristers should sing every day in the chapel. Today, the world famous King's College Choir, comprising 14 choral scholars from the college and 16 choristers from King's College School, sing here daily except Monday, during the university term. Visitors are welcome to attend services. The Christmas Eve Festival of Nine Lessons and Carols, established in 1928, is broadcast around the world every year.

Clare College

Leave King's by the gate north of the chapel. On the left is ★ **Clare ❸**, second oldest of the colleges, founded as University Hall in 1326. Twelve years later it was rescued from poverty and refounded by Lady Elizabeth de Clare, granddaughter of Edward I. Rebuilt periodically from 1638–1719, the buildings of **Old Court**, influenced by Christopher Wren, are remarkably unified, and give more the impression of an elegant palace than an institution. Beyond the college buildings **Clare Bridge**, the oldest remaining bridge of the colleges, provides good views of the river, where punts drift by, and the glorious Fellows' Garden (seldom open to the public). The curious sixth ball on the left parapet, with a segment cut off, attracts much attention.

Leaving Clare by the main entrance, turn left. The elaborately carved gateway on the right is the entrance to the **Old Schools ❹**, originally comprising some of the first university buildings and the former Old Court of King's College. Today the buildings are used as university offices. Beyond the end of the lane, on the left, is ★ **Trinity Hall ❺**, one of the smaller and more intimate colleges. This was founded in 1350 by Bishop Bateman of Norwich with the purpose of providing a new body of clergy and lawyers following the ravages of the Black Death in the summer of 1347. It is still regarded as the lawyers' college. Front Court beyond the entrance was built in the late 14th century, but was refaced in stone four centuries later. Through the screens passage the delightful **Tudor brick library**, which has survived almost intact, contains Jacobean desks and some of the original books, still chained for security (no admission). The little wooden door half way up the building may have been connected to an elevated walkway to the Master's Lodge. The College and Fellows' Gardens lie beyond Library Court, flanking the river.

Trinity Hall: Tudor brick library

From the main Trinity Hall entrance take Senate House Passage diagonally to the right. A short way down on the left the domed ★ **Gate of Honour ❻** of **Gonville and Caius College** is one of the earliest Renaissance stone structures of the city. Dr John Caius (pronounced 'Keys'), former student and famous physician, refounded his old college in 1565, built a new court (visible if the gate is open) and created the three gates of Humility, Virtue and Honour, symbolising the ideal progress of a student through his College. The Gate of Humility, forming the main Trinity Street entrance, was re-sited in the Master's garden in the 19th century; the Gate of Virtue is the great arch between Caius Court and Tree Court (seen later on the walk from the main entrance). Undergraduates of the college still pass through the Gate of Honour to receive their degrees at the graduation ceremonies at the ★ **Senate House ❼** opposite. The second of James Gibbs' masterpieces (1722–30), this elegant classical building is the meeting place of the governing body of the university. West of the Senate House, the former Squire Law Library is now home to **Gonville and Caius College Library** (no access), containing one of the finest collections of medieval books in Cambridge.

Gonville and Caius College: Gate of Honour

Until the construction of the Senate House, degrees were awarded at the university **Church of Great St Mary's** (St Mary the Great) ❽, reached by crossing Trinity Street at the end of Senate House Passage. Many great clerics have preached here, including the Protestant martyrs, Latimer, Ridley and Cranmer, who were all burned at the stake under Queen Mary. University sermons can be heard here on Sunday evenings during the academic term. Visitors willing to climb 123 steps up the tower will be rewarded by a fine ★ **panorama** of the colleges and town.

Gonville and Caius College Library

19

Graduation ceremony outside the Senate House

Cambridge University Press Book Shop

The church is regarded as the very centre of Cambridge, all distances being measured from the base of the right-hand buttress. A former regulation stipulated that all students had to live within 3 miles (5km) of this landmark.

Take Trinity Street to the north of the church, passing the **Cambridge University Press Book Shop** ❾ (opposite the Senate House), the oldest bookshop site in Britain, dating from the 16th century. Further along on the left, the entrance of **Gonville and Caius**, more familiarly known as 'Caius', leads into Tree Court, designed in Loire *chateau* style by Alfred Waterhouse in 1869. The Gate of Virtue leads to Caius Court (*see page 19*).

Trinity College: the Gatehouse

Further along Trinity Street it is hard to miss the Great Gate of ★★★ **Trinity College** ❿, largest and richest of them all. Just six weeks before he died in 1547, Henry VIII founded the college by amalgamating the existing King's Hall and Michael House, and enriching them with endowments from the dissolved monasteries. The **Great Gate**, built between 1490 and 1535, bears the arms of Edward III, who founded King's Hall, along with those of his six sons. The blank shield belongs to the son who died before the arms could be granted. Occupying centre stage is a statue of Henry VIII holding a chair leg, the lost sceptre having been the target of a student prank. The story goes that the apple tree to the right of the forecourt comes from the seed of the famous tree whose apple dropped on Isaac Newton's head and inspired his theory of gravity. Trinity has produced a wealth of other illustrious men, including over 20 Nobel prize-winners, six prime ministers, several famous poets and philosophers (Byron, Tennyson, Bertrand Russell, Francis Bacon), and various royals including Edward VII, George VI and the current Prince of Wales.

Famous former students

The 16th-century **Great Court**, impressive for sheer size and grandeur rather than architectural homogeneity, is the largest academic quadrangle in Europe. This is the scene of the 'Great Court Run' when students attempt to run the perimeter of the quadrangle (380 yards/347.5m) within the time taken for the clock to strike 12 (43 seconds). The only one to achieve this feat was the Olympic runner, Lord Burghley, in 1927. The oldest feature is King Edward's Tower (1428) on the north range, built as the gateway to King's Hall. This originally stood about 20 metres south of its present position. To the right of it, the late Gothic **Chapel** was begun in the reign of Mary Tudor, daughter of Henry VIII, in 1555. The antechapel houses imposing statues of celebrated Trinity alumni, including Newton, Tennyson and Bacon, and the carved names of members of the college killed in both World Wars. The late Elizabethan carved fountain in the centre of the court used to supply the college with water via a conduit laid by Franciscan friars in 1325.

Trinity's Great Court and fountain

The Hall

21

The large ivy-clad building on the west range of the court is the Master's Lodge, the Master here being the only one in Cambridge who is nominated by royalty. From Great Court an old doorway leads to the screens passage, on the right of which is the fine Elizabethan dining **Hall** (3–5pm daily). On the entrance side the intricately carved Minstrels Gallery has large panels on the upper floor which can be removed when the choir sings here during feasts. Beyond the screens passage Nevile's Court (1612) is a cloistered quadrangle flanked on the west side by the ★★ **Wren Library** ⓫ (1695) (university terms, Monday to Friday noon–2pm, Saturday 10.30am–12.30pm), designed as a gift to the college by Sir Christopher Wren and one of the finest classical buildings in England. The four statues surmounting the library represent the disciplines of Divinity, Law, Physics and Mathematics. The perfectly proportioned library interior contains many rare manuscripts and first editions, with works by Shakespeare, Milton and Bertrand Russell. Sculptures of Trinity men include a statue of Byron intended for Westminster Abbey but rejected on the grounds of the poet's immorality.

Leave the college by the south arcade into New Court, and turn right for The Backs. If access to visitors is barred turn right out of Trinity main gate, right into Trinity Lane and right again for Garret Hostel Lane. Cross the bridge and join the walk at the end of the lane, by Queens' Road.

★★★ **The Backs** ⓬, laid out in the late 17th and early 18th century, are the lawns, meadows and gardens owned by the colleges which back on to the river. These look particularly fine in spring when crocuses, daffodils and tulips provide a riot of colour. The colleges, linked by

King's College Chapel from The Backs

bridges to the Backs, look quite different from this aspect and a walk along the footpaths gives you an idea of the wealth of architectural styles. Trinity Backs command good views, foliage permitting, of St John's neo-Gothic New Court facade (*see Route 3, page 30*) and the west side of the Wren Library.

Take the avenue of limes, crossing Trinity Bridge, and turn left just after the wrought iron gate. Continue along the footpath, crossing the lane. You can soon see **Clare Memorial Court** across the main Queens' Road, built in 1924 in memory of members of the college killed in World War I. The tower beyond it belongs to the **University Library**, home to 92 miles of shelved books. As a copyright library it receives, free of charge, a copy of every book published in the UK. To your left the gateway leads along an avenue to Clare Bridge and college. Keeping on the path, you are soon greeted by the most familiar ★★★ **vista** in Cambridge: King's College Chapel and the Gibbs' Building, seen across Scholars' Piece and the meadows, where cattle graze in summer.

Queens' College

Beyond the back entrance of King's, veer left into Queens' Green for ★★ **Queens' College** 🄳 (normally daily 10.15am–12.45pm and 1.45–4.30pm), heralded by the modern Lyon Court (1989). For the main college entrance follow the path to Silver Street, turn left, cross the bridge and take the first left turn into Queens' Lane. Originally founded in 1446, the college was reestablished by Margaret of Anjou, wife of Henry VI, in 1448, and then by Queen Elizabeth Woodville, wife of Edward IV, in 1465 – hence the plural spelling of 'Queens'.

Cloister Court and the Mathematical Bridge

The gateway leads into **Old Court**, one of the finest examples of a medieval quadrangle. The sundial on the north range dates from 1642. Erasmus, first teacher of Greek at Cambridge, occupied rooms in the turret in the southwest corner of the court from 1511–14. Beyond the passage lies the enchanting **Cloister Court**, flanked on the right by the half-timbered Tudor president's lodge and gallery. This makes a perfect setting for the Shakespeare performances which take place here on summer evenings. The Cam divides the college into two parts and is spanned by what is often mistakenly called the **Mathematical Bridge**. Contrary to popular belief this was not designed by Newton, nor was it built without the use of bolts – it was in fact constructed in 1904 as an identical replacement to the original (1749), using bolts at the main joints.

Return to Cloister Court, and take the small passageway in the far left corner for Walnut Tree Court, and beyond the chapel to Friars' Court. The Erasmus Building, designed by Sir Basil Spence in 1959–60, was the first modern building on the Backs and hence highly controversial. Leave the college by the main entrance.

Route 2

Christ's Fellows' Building

Where Town Meets Gown

Christ's – St Andrew the Great – Emmanuel – Science Museums – Bene't Street Church – Corpus Christi – Pembroke – Peterhouse – Fitzwilliam Museum – Botanic Gardens *See map, pages 14–15*

23

This route takes you through the heart of the city, where the busy streets contrast with the hallowed courts and tranquil gardens of medieval colleges.

The walk starts in the heart of the city at **Christ's College ⓮** on St Andrew's Street. First established in 1437 as 'God's House' on a site by the river, the foundation was forced to move when Henry VI reclaimed the land to build King's College Chapel. The present site was acquired and the college was refounded as 'Christ's' in 1505 by Lady Margaret Beaufort, mother of Henry VII. Her statue occupies a niche on the gatehouse, above the Beaufort coat of arms. The curious animals either side, with the body of an antelope and the head of a goat, are mythological beasts called yales.

First Court, the oldest part of the college, retains buildings from the original God's House, but the clunch (local limestone) and red brick was almost entirely refaced in stone in the 18th century. The foundress lived for a while in the first floor rooms of what is now the Master's lodge, conspicuous for the brightly painted Beaufort coat of arms below the bay window.

The archway in the far right-hand corner leads past the hall into Second Court. On the far side the ★ **Fellows' Building** (1642), traditionally attributed but probably wrongly to Inigo Jones, is a splendid example of 17th-

Christ's: a meeting of minds

Church of St Andrew the Great

Emmanuel College

Pool in The Paddock

century English classicism. If the gate is open go through to the ★ **Fellows' Garden** (weekdays 10.30am–12.30pm and 2–4pm), a magical oasis in the middle of the city. Milton's Mulberry Tree, where the poet is said to have sat composing verse, was one of several of the species planted by James I in 1608 (the year of Milton's birth) to stimulate the English silk industry. The pool, hidden to the right of the path at the far end, is believed to be the oldest private bathing-pool in England. The three busts represent prestigious alumni of the college, including Milton. The memorial urn contains the ashes of the author C.P. Snow, a fellow of Christ's from 1930–50. Among the more recent additions to the college is New Court, reached via the footpath beside the Fellows' Building. This staggered white building, characteristic of the 1960s, is known as Christ's 'typewriter'.

Leave the college by the main gate. On the opposite side of the road the **Church of St Andrew the Great** ⓫ contains a monument to Captain Cook, the great explorer from North Yorkshire who was murdered on Hawaii in 1779. His widow and two eldest sons are buried here. The church entrance, which is on the far side, is normally closed – to see inside ring one of the bells at the entrance opposite the Body Shop.

Further along St Andrew's Street, on the left opposite Downing Street, is **Emmanuel College** ⓰, familiarly known as 'Emma'. Built on the site of a Dominican Friary dissolved by Henry VIII, this was the first Protestant college, founded in 1584 by Sir Walter Mildmay. Chancellor of the Exchequer to Elizabeth I and a renowned Puritan, his intent was to create a college that would become 'a seed-plot of learned men' for the recently founded Protestant church. The movement to persecute religious dissidents under Charles I led many English Puritan clergy to leave the country for New England. Of the first 100 graduates to settle there, one-third were members of Emmanuel. Among them was John Harvard, who founded and gave his name to the first university of America.

The classical ★ **Chapel**, facing you as you enter Front Court, was designed by Christopher Wren in 1666–77. The late 19th-century stained glass windows depict men of the Church and Reformation, among them John Harvard. Since there was no portrait to go by, the depiction is partly based on his Cambridge contemporary, John Milton.

New Court, north of Front Court (through the gate marked E), is, despite its name, the oldest part of the college. To the right the Old Library was the original chapel. Returning to Front Court take the passageway in the far left-hand corner to the spacious college garden, known as **The Paddock**, featuring fine plants and trees, and a large pool where the Dominican friars used to fish.

Opposite Emmanuel, Downing Street is home to university science departments and museums. The Downing and New Museums sites are uninspiring architecturally, but the museums (free of charge) have some fascinating exhibits. The imposing Edwardian buildings a short way down on the left house the Museum of Geology and the Museum of Archaeology and Anthropology. The **Sedgwick Museum of Geology** ⓱ (Monday to Friday 9am–1pm and 2–5pm, Saturday 10am–1pm) contains rare and curious specimens of fossils, minerals, rocks and plant material, and includes Britain's oldest intact geological collection. The **Museum of Archaeology and Anthropology** ⓲ (Monday to Friday 2–4pm, Saturday 10am–12.30pm) is devoted to world prehistory and local archaeology with sections on Prehistoric Europe, The Americas, Africa and Asia, as well as Britain and a special section on Cambridgeshire.

Museum of Zoology

25

Further along Downing Street, on the right, the New Museums site was built on land formerly occupied by the Botanical Gardens. The **Museum of Zoology** ⓳ (Monday to Friday 2.15– 4.45pm) has a fascinating collection of skeletons, fossils, reptiles, insects, shells and coral, as well as a couple of live pythons. At the entrance the 'Beagle' fish and rhea skeleton were collected by Darwin on his 1831 voyage on HMS Beagle.

Take the first turning on the right for Free School Lane where the **Whipple Science Museum** ⓴ (Monday to Friday 2–4pm) houses a collection of scientific and navigational instruments dating back to the 14th century. Further down on the right the old **Cavendish Laboratories** (1847) became internationally famous for the splitting of the atom in 1932 by Ernest Rutherford and for the discovery of DNA in the 1950s by Crick and Watson. It is named after Henry Cavendish (1731–1810), a physicist and chemist who pursued science as a recluse and acquired fame for determining the composition of air and for measuring the density and mass of the Earth (at 6,000 million million million tonnes). In 1974 the Cavendish was moved to Madingley Road in west Cambridge.

Ceiling decor at The Eagle

Visible at the end of Free School Lane, the Saxon tower of **St Bene't's Church** ㉑ is the city's oldest architectural feature, built in about 1025 during the reign of King Canute. The rest of the church was added between the 13th and 15th centuries. For 300 years it was used as the chapel for neighbouring Corpus Christi College and many of its priests have been Fellows of the College.

Over the road the **Eagle pub** ㉒, good for real ale and food, was formerly a coaching inn. The Air Force Bar ceiling bears the candle-smoke and lipstick signatures of British and American pilots who patronised the pub during World War II.

THE EAGLE

HOME COOKED FOOD
COLD BUFFET
COURTYARD
FINE ALES & WINES

LICENSED HOURS 11.00am–11.00pm DAILY
12.00am–3.00pm 7.00pm–10.30pm SUN DAY
(USE OF COURT YARD NOT PERMITTED)
AFTER 10·30pm

NO PARKING

St Catherine's College

Corpus Christi:
Old Court doorway

26

From Bene't Street a path by the churchyard leads to the former entrance of **Corpus Cristi** ㉓. Dating from 1352, the college was founded by local trade guilds and hence is the only Oxbridge college to have been set up by townspeople. ★★ **Old Court**, where you enter, was the first complete college court at Cambridge and, apart from the addition of buttresses, dormers and chimneys, looks much as it would have done in the 14th century. Having escaped the 18th-century trend of stone refacing, it is one of the finest examples of a medieval court in Cambridge. This was the only court at Corpus Christi until the 19th century, when the college was substantially enlarged by the Gothic Revival **New Court** (for access take the archway on the far side of Old Court). It was designed in the 1820s by William Wilkins, who also masterminded the neo-Gothic screen and hall-range of King's College. The library on the south side contains a priceless collection of manuscripts and medieval books, many from dissolved monasteries, collected by Matthew Parker, Master of the College in 1544 and Archbishop of Canterbury under Elizabeth I. A clever and very curious individual, with a long nose, he gave his name to the expression 'nosey parker'.

Leave Corpus by the main entrance on Trumpington Street. Across the road you can see **St Catherine's College** ㉔ (commonly known as 'Catz'), founded in 1473 by the Provost of King's. Among its more famous alumni were John Addenbrooke, founder of the county hospital, and William Wotton (1666–1727), the infant prodigy who was versed in Latin, Greek and Hebrew at the age of five and came up to Cambridge when he was nine!

Next to Corpus Christi, the **Church of St Botolph** ㉕ was built in the 14th century near the Trumpington Gate. Travellers used to stop here to say a prayer before em-

Church of
St Botolph

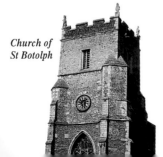

barking on their journey to London, and to give thanks on their return. Cross Botolph Lane for Fitzbilles, famous for cakes and Chelsea buns.

Pembroke College ㉖, beyond Pembroke Street, is best known for its ★ **chapel** (turn right on entry). Built in 1663–5 this was the first work to be completed by Sir Christopher Wren and also the first classical-style building in Cambridge or Oxford. The original chapel, which was the first of all the colleges, occupied what is now known as the Old Library (left on entry). Wren's chapel was funded by his uncle, Bishop Matthew Wren (see also Peterhouse below) who had been imprisoned by Cromwell in the Tower of London for 18 years and gave the chapel in thanks for his safe release. The building beyond it is Alfred Waterhouse's Library (1875–7) with a statue in front of a toga-clad William Pitt the Younger, who came up to Pembroke at 14, was a Member of Parliament at 18 and became Prime Minister at 24. The politician occupied the same rooms as Thomas Gray, the poet, who was driven away from Peterhouse by a series of student pranks.

Pembroke College: the chapel

Almost opposite Pembroke is **Peterhouse** ㉗, oldest of all the Cambridge colleges, founded by Hugh de Balsham, the Bishop of Ely, in 1286. The oldest building is the much altered and renovated Hall, on the left of Old Court, whose interior was Gothicised with fine woodwork by George Gilbert Scott (1839–97). But the outstanding architectural feature of the college is the chapel on the east side, an essentially Gothic building that successfully incorporates Renaissance detail. This was one of several buildings constructed under the mastership of Matthew Wren (Christopher Wren's uncle – *see above*) who was Master here from 1625–34. Peterhouse alumni have included famous scientists such as Henry Cavendish (*see page 25*) and Sir Frank Whittle, inventor of the jet engine. The neo-Palladian Burrough's Building to the north of the chapel was designed in 1736 by Sir James Burrough, Master of Gonville and Caius.

Peterhouse

A covered gallery from the college (closed to the public) links it to **St Mary The Less** ㉘, which was the parish church and college chapel from 1284–1632. Before being rebuilt in 1340–52 the church was called St Peter-without-Trumpington-Gate, being sited beyond the gate which originally stood on the south side of the city. The church stands on St Mary's Lane, a narrow street bordered by 16th to 18th-century cottages and the delightfully overgrown churchyard.

St Mary the Less

Leaving Peterhouse, turn right for the ★★★ **Fitzwilliam Museum** ㉙ (Tuesday to Saturday, all galleries open 10am–5pm, subject to staff availability). This is one of the

oldest museums in the country, containing a remarkably rich and varied collection, and certainly one of the finest outside London. The museum was founded in the early 19th century by the 7th Viscount Fitzwilliam, who bequeathed his priceless collection of paintings, books, prints and illuminated manuscripts to the university and financed a museum to house it. The formidable, temple-like building was designed by George Basevi in 1834 and has been extended at various stages to accommodate the many gifts and bequests.

There are now 46 galleries and plans for a large new extension. The lower galleries house a wide-ranging collection of antiquities, sculpture, sarcophagi, paintings and pottery from Ancient Egypt and Western Asia; vases, bronzes, sculpture and jewellery from Greece and Rome; ceramics from the Far East, England and Europe; English glass, ancient coins, illuminated manuscripts and portrait miniatures, as well as the Henderson collection of armour. The upper galleries are devoted to a very extensive collection of paintings, including masterpieces by Italian Renaissance painters, Flemish and Dutch artists, French Impressionists and English landscape and portrait painters, as well as a wide range of 20th-century art; furniture and rugs also form an integrated part of the displays. Temporary exhibitions are shown at the museum throughout the year.

The Cambridge University ★★ **Botanic Gardens** ㉚ (March to September, daily 10am–6pm; February and October 10am–5pm; January, November and December 10am–4pm) provide an ideal antidote to a surfeit of sightseeing. The gardens lie half a mile (800m) along Trumpington Road. Turn right out of the Fitzwilliam Museum and take the second main road on the left for the Bateman Street entrance.

28

The Botanic Gardens: pond life

Until 1831 the gardens occupied a site in the town centre and many of the plants were grown for medicinal purposes. The present location covers about 40 acres (16 hectares), with some 8,000 species of plants. One of the finest botanic gardens in the country, this has magnificent species of trees, shrubs and plants and provides a brilliant display of colour all year round. Features of the 19th-century Garden include the beautiful Lake, Stream and Water Garden, the Rock Garden and the Mediterranean Gardens. Among the 20th-century additions are the Ecological Area, with wild British plants, the Chronological Bed, with plants ranging from ancient classical and medieval times to species recently introduced to the UK, the Scented Garden, the colourful Winter Garden and the Glasshouses, with their intriguing collections of tropical and subtropical plants.

Route 3

St John's College

Colleges, Cam and Jesus Green

St John's – Church of the Holy Sepulchre – the Union
Society – Magdalene College – Kettle's Yard – Folk
Museum – River Cam and Jesus Green – Jesus College
– Sidney Sussex *See map, pages 14–15*

29

This route explores the major colleges in the northern part
of the city, taking in modern art, Victorian folklore and
a walk beside the River Cam.

The walk starts at the Gate Tower of ★★★ St John's ③,
a suitably ornate entrance to a college which is only chal-
lenged by Trinity for size and grandeur. The Gate Tower
(1516) bears the coat of arms of Lady Margaret Beaufort, mother of Henry VII, who founded the college. Her
coat of arms also decorates Christ's Gate Tower, another
of her foundations (*see page 23*). Lady Margaret was per-
suaded to found St John's by her confessor, John Fisher,
'the saintliest bishop in Christendom' who was executed
for refusing to acknowledge Henry VIII as supreme head
of the Church. Fisher was one of the university's great
benefactors and, after Lady Margaret died in 1509, he took
over the running of the college. It was finally established
in 1511 on the site of a 13th-century hospital, run by the
monks of St John. A statue of the saint, with his poisoned
cup and an eagle at his feet, stands above the coat of arms.

    First Court, built in 1511–20, formed the original col-
lege. During the Civil War, the college's royalist sympathies led to the expulsion of many of the Fellows and the
court was used as a prison by Oliver Cromwell. The original buildings are preserved, though the south range was
ashlar-faced in 1772–5 and the sense of architectural unity

*St John's: grotesque face on
Shrewsbury Tower*

St John's Dining Hall

The Bridge of Sighs

was broken by the grandiose neo-Gothic **Chapel** (Monday to Friday 9am–4pm, Saturday 9am–12pm) which replaced the old chapel in the 1860s. Inspired by the Sainte-Chapelle Chapel in Paris, this was the work of the great Gothic Revivalist architect, Sir George Gilbert Scott. Every year on Ascension Day at noon, St John's College choir sing an Ascension carol from the top of the 163-ft (42.5-m) high chapel tower. The choristers, like those of King's, have achieved international renown through recitals, recordings and concert tours. Visitors can hear them sing at evensong, normally held in the chapel from Tuesday to Sunday during the university term.

The finely carved doorway, surmounted by a statue of Lady Margaret, leads to the **Dining Hall**, hung with portraits of the foundress, benefactors and illustrious members of John's. Featuring among them are the poet William Wordsworth, the statesmen Castlereagh, Palmerston and Wilberforce, and a number of distinguished scientists and ecclesiastics. Beyond the screens passage lies the beautiful Tudor brick **Second Court**, built in 1598–1602. The **Shrewsbury Tower** on the far side bears a statue of Mary, Countess of Shrewsbury, who financed its construction. On the north side the Long Gallery (148ft/39.5m), now the Combination Room, was used during World War II for a conference when the D-Day landings were planned. A magnificent wood-panelled room, it is normally only lit by candles. In Chapel Court, adjoining Second Court, the highly acclaimed **New Library** (1994), in the form of a cross, was built to blend with the neo-Tudor range.

Beyond the Shrewsbury Tower lies **Third Court**, whose first building was the College Library (1624), on the right. A gateway leads to the **Bridge of Sighs** (1831), inspired by its Venetian namesake, and built to link the older buildings of the college to New Court. The bridge is best viewed from **Kitchen Bridge**, a fine early 18th-century structure, which also bears the less pedestrian name of Wren Bridge, after the famous architect who submitted a design which was never used.

Around the beginning of the 18th century, a sharp rise in student numbers necessitated considerable expansion. The result was **New Court** (1825–31), the biggest individual building that any college had constructed to date. Basically classical in plan, it is elaborated with Gothic detail and nicknamed 'The Wedding Cake'. The building is best admired from a distance, ideally across the lawn from the Backs. The award-winning Cripps Building (1967), reached via the archway opposite the gate of North Court, stands in stark modern contrast to the older buildings of the college. Beyond it to the west, the School of Pythagoras dates from the end of the 12th century and as such is the oldest private house in the county.

Return to the college entrance and turn left down St John's Street. At the end of the street, over the road, the ★ **Church of the Holy Sepulchre** ㉜ (daily 10am–5pm), or Round Church, is one of five surviving churches in England with a round nave. It was built in the 12th century but substantially altered three centuries later. In 1841 a Cambridge society, intent on restoring the church to its original form, destroyed most of the 15th-century fabric.

The alleyway beside the church leads to the **Cambridge Union Society** ㉝, the debating forum of many a budding politician. Designed by Alfred Waterhouse in 1866 and since enlarged, it has seen many years of heated debate among students and visiting speakers.

Cambridge Union Society

From the Round Church go west along Bridge Street, which follows the line of the Roman road up to the bridge over the River Cam. The river was forded here by the Romans; and later a wooden Saxon bridge was built called Grontabridge, meaning 'swampy river bridge'. **Magdalene College** ㉞, on the right, was originally founded by Henry VI as a hostel for student Benedictine monks, sited north of the river to be well away from the temptations of the town. The college fell into decline during the Dissolution, but was established as Magdalene (pronounced 'Maudlin') College in 1542 by Henry VIII's Lord Chancellor, Thomas, Lord Audley of Audley End. For his descendants Audley procured the entitlement to the nomination of the Master of the College – a tradition which still carries on today. The college showpiece is the ★ **Pepys Library** (Monday to Saturday 11.30am–12.30pm and 2.30–3.30pm, winter afternoons only), in the Pepys Building of Second Court. A member of Magdalene, Samuel Pepys bequeathed his 3,000-book library to the college in 1703. The greatest treasure is the original manuscript of his famous diary, recording daily life in the 1660s.

Magdalene College: the Pepys Building

Exiting the college, cross over Magdalene Street and turn right. The 16th-century and later cottages on this side of the street also belong to the college. At the traffic lights turn left, cross the road at the next lights and take the path over the green to ★★ **Kettle's Yard** ㉟ (daily except Monday 2–4pm). More of a home than a museum, the house used to belong to Jim Ede, Tate Gallery curator and friend of many leading artists of the early 20th century. In 1956 he came to Cambridge 'looking for a stately home', instead of which he restored and remodelled four derelict cottages. This delightful setting became the home of his collection of paintings, sculpture, ceramics and other *objets d'art*. Works by Ben Nicholson, Alfred Wallis, Christopher Wood, Constantin Brancusi, Henry Moore, Barbara Hepworth and others can be enjoyed in the comfort and intimacy of the house. The new extension holds temporary art exhibitions.

Kettle's Yard exhibit

Beyond it, an exit brings you on to Castle Hill. Turn right, passing on the corner the **Folk Museum** ㊱, within one of the oldest private dwellings in Cambridge. Quaint rooms include a Fen display, with drainage tools, wicker eel snares and viscious mantraps used to catch poachers.

The Quayside

Retrace your steps down Magdalene Street and over the bridge turn left on to **The Quayside** ㊲. This is a favourite spot in summer when café tables are laid out by the river and punts are hired out for trips along The Backs or northwards to Jesus Lock. Follow the boardwalk by the river, savouring the views across the water to the secluded Magdalene Fellows' garden. This brings you to **Jesus Green** ㊳, a large open space providing a rural haven close to the centre, with a huge open-air pool, tennis courts and a bowling green. Keep beside the river as far as the bridge, then veer right onto the footpath crossing the green, along the avenue lined by plane trees. At the end of the path Victoria Road divides Jesus Green from **Midsummer Common** ㊴, where a fair has been held in midsummer since the 13th century. Turn right along Victoria Road. The spacious grounds and buildings to your right are part of **Jesus College** ㊵, whose main entrance is on Jesus Lane.

Jesus College:
bronze horse (above) and Tudor
Gate House detail (below)

The Bishop of Ely, John Alcock, founded the college in 1496 on the site of the suppressed Nunnery of St Radegund, which had been built by the Normans. James I, impressed by the tranquil surroundings of the college, commented that, were he to choose, he would 'pray at King's, dine at Trinity, and study and sleep at Jesus'. A walled passageway known as 'The Chimney' links the gateway on Jesus Lane to the **Tudor Gate House**, which features Bishop Alcock's rebus of three cocks' heads. In First Court the **bronze horse** on the lawn is one of several striking modern sculptures offsetting the traditional

Tudor buildings. Take the central archway on the right range for the beautiful **Cloister Court**, which formed part of the old nunnery. The nuns' church, rebuilt in the 13th century, was far too large for a college which originally consisted of six Fellows and a handful of scholars. The western part of the nave was therefore converted into chambers, later to become the Master's Lodge, and the Chapter House was destroyed except for the entrance wall, whose beautiful ★ **Early English arches** (c1230) were discovered under plasterwork in 1893. The enchanting ★★ **Chapel** is the oldest building of any Cambridge college, the nave dating from about 1200. The church was restored by the Victorian Gothicist, Pugin, and the new ceilings were designed and windows reglazed by Morris & Co. The chapel has memorials to the college's two most distinguished members: Thomas Cranmer, Archbishop of Canterbury, burned at the stake in Oxford in 1556; and the poet, Samuel Taylor Coleridge.

Early English arches

Exiting the college, turn right along Jesus Lane. Cross the road by the beautiful Queen Anne red-brick house and continue along the lane, passing on the right a white building with an incongruous Ionic portico. Built to house a mock Roman Bath, this became the political Pitt Club which today shares the building with a pizzeria.

33

At the junction turn left for **Sidney Sussex College** ㊶. This is one of the smallest colleges of Cambridge, founded in 1596 on the site of a dissolved Franciscan friary. Its most famous member was Oliver Cromwell, who came here from his grammar school in Huntingdon in 1616. University life, however, was cut short the following year when his father died and he returned home to support his family. In 1643 Cromwell returned to Cambridge, looting the colleges (whose sympathies lay with the King) and requisitioning some of their courts as barracks. Sidney Sussex is the last resting place of **Cromwell's head**, which had had a rough ride since its burial in Westminster Abbey in 1658. Following the restoration of Charles II, Cromwell's relics were exhumed, hung up at Tyburn, and his head then impaled on a spike on Wesminster Hall for 20 years. The skull, which blew down in a storm, was smuggled away and passed through various hands over the centuries before being offered to the college in 1960. It was buried in the ante-chapel floor, but the exact position remains a secret. A portrait of Cromwell hangs in the dining hall, and tradition has it that he is covered by a curtain when a toast is drunk to the Queen at college feasts.

Sydney Sussex cloisters

Turn left out of the college and take the first street on your right which is Market Street, one of the oldest shopping streets in Cambridge. This comes out at Market Hill, heart of the city and scene of the colourful market.

Punts at Scudamore's Boat Yard

A skilled punter in action

Rupert Brooke

Byron's Pool

Punting to Grantchester

2 miles (3km) south of Cambridge.

Punting upstream along the tranquil River Cam or strolling along the riverside meadows are the most agreeable means of getting to the village of Grantchester. The footpath starts at Grantchester Street in Newnham, southwest of the city centre. Punts can be hired, with or without chauffeur, from Scudamore's Boat Yard (*see page 74*).

A skilled punter should be able to get to Grantchester in 1½ hours or less. One warning, though: those unaccustomed to the pole-manoeuvred boats should beware of the deep sections of the river and the mud of the riverbed where the pole can get stuck.

The village on the river was immortalised by Rupert Brooke, the poet who wrote movingly of the futility of war and died in World War I at the age of 28. A student of King's College, Brooke fell in love with Grantchester and spent much of his time here, studying, swimming, walking barefoot and boating to Cambridge. The last two lines of his eulogy, *The Old Vicarage, Grantchester* (1912), written in nostalgic mood from a Berlin café, still reverberate in the village lanes:

Stands the Church clock at ten to three
And is there honey still for tea?

It is believed the clock had broken in Brooke's day – if this was not the case, it was altered to stand at ten to three for several years as a memorial to the poet. The clock today is fully functional but there is still honey for tea beneath the apple trees in the Orchard Garden.

During the idyllic pre-war period this was a favourite haunt of Brooke and a group of friends, who became known as the Grantchester Group or the 'neo-pagans': the philosophers, Bertrand Russell and Ludwig Wittgenstein; the writers, E.M. Forster and Virginia Woolf; the economist, Maynard Keynes; and the artist, Augustus John. Brooke lodged at Orchard House in 1909, then later moved to the Old Vicarage next door, which is now the home of the Conservative politician and best-selling novelist, Jeffrey Archer.

Grantchester's appeal today lies in the river setting and literary connections. In spring and summer the village draws a steady stream of visitors to its pubs, tea garden and riverside walks. Brooke, who was buried in an olive grove on the island of Skiros in Greece, is commemorated on a war memorial in the churchyard, along with other war victims.

Byron's Pool, where the poet swam during his student days at Trinity, lies about half a mile south of the village, and is reached by a footpath to the right, just after the river bridge on the road to Trumpington.

Excursions from Cambridge

Ely Cathedral and gargoyle

Ely

16 miles (25km) north of Cambridge, via the A10.
Derived from the Saxon *elge*, or eel district, Ely was formerly an inaccessible island, surrounded by marshland which seethed with fish and eels. Following the reclamation of the Fenland in the 17th century (*see page 8*), it developed into a thriving market town.

35

Rising shiplike above the city and surrounding Fens is the great ★★★ **Cathedral of Ely** (Easter to October daily 7am–7pm, winter Monday to Friday 7.30am–6pm, Sunday 7.30am–5pm). The first religious institution here was a Benedictine monastery for monks and nuns, founded in 673 by St Ethelreda, daughter of Anna, King of the East Angles. This was destroyed by invading Danes in 869, but a new monastery rose from the ruins 100 years later. It was here that Hereward the Wake, 'the Last Englishman', held out against the William the Conqueror until his final defeat in 1071. Ten years later the Norman Abbot of Ely, Simeon, laid the foundation stone of the cathedral.

The nave and the timber octagon

The magnificent interior, with its 250-ft (76-m) long nave, reflects various architectural styles, from Norman, through the Early English, Decorated and Perpendicular Gothic styles to the early Renaissance. The crowning glory is the **timber octagon**, supported by eight columns and crowned by the seemingly weightless lantern tower. This masterpiece of engineering was designed by the Sacrist, Alan of Walsingham, following the collapse of the Norman tower in 1322. The **Lady Chapel** (1321–53), the largest in the country, formerly glowed with medieval stained-glass windows, but these, along with the heads of the statuettes, were destroyed during the Reformation. At the east end of the cathedral, Bishop Alcock's Chantry, commemorating the founder of Jesus College, Cambridge,

Stained Glass Museum

is decorated with a wealth of Gothic ornament. Bishop West's Chantry, on the other side, is also Gothic in form but the ceiling shows the Renaissance style emerging.

The **Stained Glass Museum**, occupying a splendid new location in the South Triforium, was founded to rescue, preserve and display stained glass windows threatened by church redundancies. The museum traces the history of stained glass and demonstrates glass-making techniques.

Next to St Mary's Church, west of the Cathedral, the black and white timbered building housing the tourist office was the **residence of Oliver Cromwell** from 1636–47. A video covers his life and times, and various rooms are open to the public, including a Civil War Exhibition, Cromwell's Study and a haunted bedroom.

Oliver Cromwell and his wife

American Military Cemetery

4 miles (6.5 km) west of Cambridge, on the A1303. Open daily 8am–6pm (5pm off-season).

Near the quiet village of Madingley, the evocative cemetery is a tribute to the 5,000 American servicemen based in England who died during World War II. The ranks of white crosses are laid out on a landscaped hillside, with a chapel behind and a Wall of Remembrance bearing the names of the servicemen whose graves are unknown.

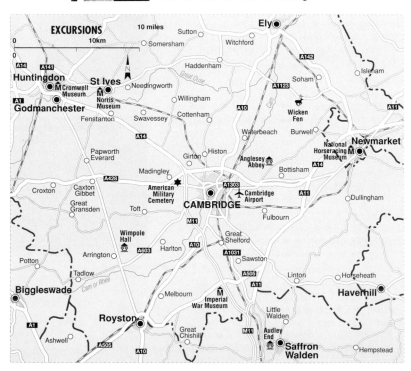

EXCURSIONS

Duxford, Imperial War Museum

8 miles (13km) south of Cambridge, off Junction 10 of the M11. Open daily mid-March to October 10am–6pm, winter 10am–4pm; tel: 01223 835000.

War Museum exhibit

Duxford Airfield, a former Battle of Britain fighter station, boasts the largest collection of historic aircraft in Europe. Housed mainly within six large exhibition buildings, displays include dramatic battlefield scenes of tanks and artillery, the reconstructed wartime Operations Room, a prototype of Concorde and a flight simulator enabling visitors to experience a Battle of Britain dogfight between a Spitfire and a Messerschmitt. The new **American Air Museum** houses Duxford's outstanding collection of historic American combat aircraft. Major air shows, involving Spitfires and Mustangs, are staged during the summer.

Wimpole Hall

8 miles (13km) southwest of Cambridge via the A603.

Until 1976, when it became a National Trust property, Wimpole Hall was the home of Elsie Bambridge, daughter of Rudyard Kipling. She and her husband, Captain George Bambridge, bought the neglected and empty mansion in 1938, and over the years restored and furnished the building. The original house of 1640 had seen major reconstruction in the 18th century under James Gibb, who designed the west wing, great staircase and splendid Long Library; and under Sir John Soane who designed the dramatic yellow drawing room and the bizarre Bath House. The extensive grounds incorporate the popular Home Farm, which specialises in rare breeds of animals.

37

Anglesey Abbey

6 miles (10km) northeast of Cambridge on the B1102. House: end March to mid-October, Wednesday to Sunday and Bank Holiday Monday 1–5pm; garden: 11am–5.30pm, and Monday and Tuesday July to September).

Anglesey Abbey garden

The name of the 17th-century manor house derives from the Augustinian abbey which originally occupied the site. In 1926 the property was bought by Lord Fairhaven who furnished it with his fine collection of antiques, paintings, sculpture and ceramics, and miraculously transformed the surrounding fenland into a superb garden with all the grandeur of the 18th century. Within the grounds **Lode Mill** is still in working order, grinding wheat to produce flour which visitors can buy.

Saffron Walden and Audley End

15 miles (24km) south of Cambridge via the A1301 and B184 or the M11 exit 9, northbound only, and exit 10.

It was thanks to the cloth trade and the crocus, used for orange dye and medicinal purposes, that Saffron Walden

Saffron Walden

flourished in medieval times. Today it is a delightfully unspoilt market town with a large number of old timber-framed houses, several of them decorated with ornamental plasterwork, or 'pargetting'. The huge church, which dominates the town, is a fine example of the Perpendicular style, having been designed by John Wastell, master mason of King's College Chapel in Cambridge.

Audley End House

Situated 1 mile (1.5km) west of Saffron Walden on the B1383, **Audley End House** (April to September, Wednesday to Sunday and Bank Holidays noon–6pm; grounds 10am–6pm) is a grandiose Jacobean mansion, set amid splendid parkland designed by Capability Brown. It is named after Thomas, first Lord Audley, who as Speaker of the Parliament from 1529–35 passed Acts for the Suppression of the Monasteries and was rewarded by King Henry VIII with – among other gifts – the abbey of Walden. Nothing survives of this monument and it was Thomas Howard, Earl of Suffolk and Lord Treasurer, who built the present mansion in the early 17th century. Designed to entertain the king and his court, the mansion used to be twice its present size, provoking James I's sarcastic remark: 'It is too large for a King, but might do for a Lord Treasurer'. Charles II clearly did not think so as he bought the palace in 1669 for £50,000. The 18th century saw grand changes under the great baroque architect, Sir John Vanbrugh, and later, under the leading architect and designer Robert Adam. The original facade has been retained and the Great Hall preserves its huge, elaborately carved Jacobean oak screen and hammerbeam roof. Over 30 rooms are open to the public, many restored to their former splendour.

38

Newmarket: statue of Hyperion

Newmarket

13 miles (21km) east of Cambridge via the A14.

Newmarket has been celebrated as a mecca of horse racing since James I, a passionate hunter, established a small palace here in the early 17th century. Charles I initiated a Gold Cup race here in 1634 and under Charles II, 'the father of the British turf', Newmarket became the most fashionable racecourse in the country. Today over 2,500 horses, including some of the country's most important thoroughbred studs, are trained on Newmarket Heath. In 1963 the **National Stud** (March to August and Race Days in September and October, tours by appointment only, tel: 01638 663464) was transferred to Newmarket and is now one of the principal stallion stations in Britain. The **National Horseracing Museum** (June to August daily 10am–5pm, March to June, September and November closed Mondays) charts the history of horse racing, from the patronage of Charles II to the great British jockeys of the 20th century.

Huntingdon

16 miles (26km) northwest of Cambridge, via the A14.
Huntingdon's hero is Oliver Cromwell, born here in 1599.
The little **Cromwell Museum** (open daily except Monday) is located in the Lord Protector's old Grammar School, occupying what was once an extensive medieval hospital. Among the memorabilia are portraits of Cromwell and his family, letters, books, coins and personal belongings, including his hat and walking stick.

Cromwell's hat

St Ives

14 miles (22.5km) northwest of Cambridge, via the A14 and A1096.
The town is named after St Ivo, a Persian missionary whose body is said to have been discovered by the river here in the 11th century. Formerly a busy river port, St Ives is today a small market town on the River Ouse, popular for boating and fishing. Oliver Cromwell lived here and is commemorated by a statue in Market Hill. The most notable landmark is the six-arched stone bridge supporting a small chapel which used to provide a retreat for travellers. On The Broadway, the **Norris Museum** charts the history of Huntingdonshire: prehistoric fossils, Stone Age and Roman archaeological finds, Civil War armour and present-day arts and crafts.

39

Wicken Fen

Lode Lane, Wicken, Ely. 17 miles (27km) northeast of Cambridge via the A10 and A1123. Open dawn to dusk.
Britain's oldest nature reserve, comprising 750 acres (300 hectares) of undrained marshland, gives a good idea of what the Fens would have looked like before their reclamation. Access is facilitated by a raised boardwalk and hides are provided for the study of the varied birdlife.

Wicken Fen

Tour 1

Bury St Edmunds and the Suffolk Wool Villages

Bury St Edmunds – Ickworth House – Clare – Cavendish – Long Melford – Sudbury – Lavenham

The ancient market town of Bury St Edmunds, named after the last Saxon king of East Anglia, who was slain by the Danes in 869, grew up around its Benedictine abbey. Today it is a bustling agricultural market town, with monastic ruins and a large number of historic buildings. From here it is a short drive to the picturesque villages of the Stour valley which owe their splendour to the wool trade that flourished in former times.

St Edmund's Abbey

From Cambridge take the A14 going east for ★ **Bury St Edmunds** (30 miles, 48km). In *The Pickwick Papers*, Charles Dickens, who stayed at the Angel Hotel, called Bury 'a handsome little town of thriving and cleanly appearance'. Medieval Angel Hill, where the hotel stands, is today given over to cars, and the town is a hotch-potch of architectural styles; it nevertheless retains much of its original layout, as well as 980 listed buildings and sufficient ruins to give you an idea of the scale and splendour of its former abbey.

St Edmund's Abbey derived its name from King Edmund, whose remains were brought here in 903. Pilgrims

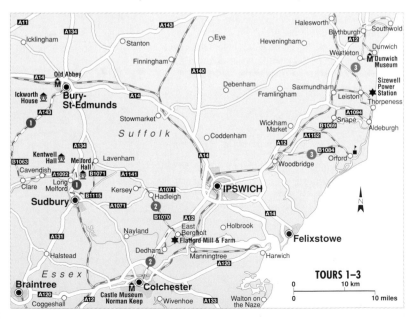

flocked to worship his shrine and in the Middle Ages the abbey became one of the richest Benedictine foundations in England. It was here in 1214 that 25 barons swore to exact their rights from King John, leading the following year to the signing of the Magna Carta. In 1539 the abbey was dissolved and most of the buildings were dismantled.

Start at the **Norman Gate Tower** (1120–48), the best preserved feature of the abbey, just south of Angel Hill. This was designed as the principal gateway to the abbey and as a belfry for the Church of St James, designated a cathedral in 1914. From the Visitor Centre, incorporated into the ruins of the great west front of the abbey, you can follow ten outdoor panels giving a brief description of the remains. The relics of the walls, arches and pillars, in some cases mere mounds of rubble, are enhanced by the setting of immaculate lawns and flower-beds. The splendid Abbey Gate, at the end of the route, replaced the original destroyed by townspeople in 1327. This leads into **Angel Hill**, venue of the Bury Fair from 1135–1871, and bordered on the south by the Athenaeum, hub of social life in Georgian times. Abbeygate Street, leading up from Angel Hill, is a bustling shopping thoroughfare, preserving some of its older facades amid newer shop fronts. The quaint Nutshell pub, on the junction with The Traverse, claims to be the smallest pub in the country. In the market square to the north, **Moyse's Hall Museum** (Monday to Saturday 10am–5pm, Sunday 2–5pm) occupies one of Britain's rare surviving Norman dwellings.

Gate Tower detail

41

Moyse's Hall Museum

From Bury take the A143 southwest towards Haverhill. At Horringer follow the signs for ★ **Ickworth House**. (Easter to October, Tuesday, Wednesday, Friday to Sunday and Bank Holiday Monday, 1–5pm). This is worth visiting for the grounds alone (daily 7am–7pm), comprising extensive gardens, woodland and parkland, with marked trails and an 8-mile (12.5-km) 'Grand Tour'. The neoclassical design of the house, comprising a huge Rotunda with wings connected by curving corridors, was conceived in 1795 by the eccentric Earl of Bristol. Today the present Marquis of Bristol occupies one wing, the other is largely redundant but plans are afoot for an arts and education centre. The Rotunda is richly furnished and has some fine paintings and silver.

Turning right out of Ickworth, follow the A143 for about 9 miles (14.5km), and turn left at Stradishall, signposted to ★ **Clare**. The village lies 5 miles (8km) along this road, its centre dominated by the splendid 'wool' Church of St Peter and St Paul. Many of its medieval houses have been preserved, and one of Suffolk's best examples of pargetting (ornamental plasterwork) can be seen on the quaint white **Ancient House** (the local museum) opposite the

Cavendish

Long Melford:
stained glass in the church

church porch. The name Clare derives from the 'clear' waters at the head of the River Stour which flows on the outskirts of the village (follow signs for the Castle Country Park). Vestiges of the Norman keep and motte (1090) and the old railway station buildings lie within the 25-acre (10-hectare) park. Over the river are the remains of an Augustinian priory, dissolved in the early 16th century.

The A1092 east of Clare, signposted at the church, leads to the village of ★ **Cavendish** (2 miles/3km). The scene of pink thatched cottages flanking the green, and the medieval church tower rising behind, is one of the most photographed in East Anglia. In more turbulent times Wat Tyler, leader of the Peasants' Revolt (1381), was killed at Smithfield by John Cavendish, arch enemy of the peasants, who lived in a house on the green. Cavendish was then beheaded in Bury St Edmunds by Tyler's supporters. On the main road the Sue Ryder Foundation, a memorial to the millions who died in World Wars I and II, was set up in 1953 to care for the sick and homeless. The neighbouring museum (daily 10am–5.30pm) tells the story of this remarkable woman and the history of her Foundation.

Continue along the A1092 for ★ **Long Melford** (4 miles/6.5km). The village derives its name from a former mill and ford and the 'Long' appropriately describing the 2-mile (3-km) road running through the village. This wide thoroughfare is lined by delightful 16th-century buildings, a remarkable number of them occupied by antique galleries and specialist shops. The **Perpendicular church**, crowning the hill above the spacious sloping green, is one of the most beautiful in Suffolk. The light-filled nave and chancel have over a hundred windows, and the north aisle has exceptionally fine stained glass, depicting friends and relatives of the Clopton family of Kentwell, the clothiers who rebuilt the church.

Kentwell Hall (tel: 01787 310207 for information), signposted from the green, is an Elizabethan red-brick manor house being renovated by a private family. Part of the interior as well as the Moat House, gardens, woods and rare breeds farm are open to the public. The hall is best known for the re-creations of everyday life in Tudor times, held on selected summer weekends.

Melford Hall (May to September, Wednesday, Thursday, Saturday, Sunday and Bank Holiday Monday; April and October Saturday and Sunday only, 2–5.30pm), whose gateway faces the village green, is a mellow red-brick Tudor mansion incorporating the remains of the medieval country retreat of the Abbots of Bury St Edmunds. Rooms open to the public include the original banqueting hall and Regency library; also memorabilia of Beatrix Potter, who was related to the family and frequently visited the hall.

Melford Hall

Sudbury lies 3 miles (5km) south of Long Melford, via the B1064 and the A131. The market town on the River Stour is best known as the birthplace of Thomas Gainsborough (1727–88), one of England's greatest portrait and landscape painters. His house at 46, Gainsborough Street, signposted from the central car parks, contains the largest collection of his works of art.

From Sudbury the route follows the B1115 and B1071 to ★★ **Lavenham** (6 miles/9.5km). This is the finest of the wool towns, preserving an extraordinary number of medieval buildings, many of them half-timbered and tilting at alarming angles. Of the 300 buildings listed as being of architectural and historical interest, most date from between 1400 and 1500 and the old centre looks much as it did then. At one time this was the 14th richest town in Britain, richer than either Lincoln or York, and famous for the blue broadcloth which it exported to Europe.

The town is heralded by the magnificent flint tower of its huge Perpendicular-style church. This was funded primarily by local cloth merchants and the top of the tower carries over 30 coats of arms of the Spring family, the principal wool merchants of the town.

The beautiful market place has one of the best examples of half-timbered buildings in the country. The **Guildhall** (daily April to October) was the meeting place of the Guild of Corpus Christi, an organisation which regulated wool production. Since the decline of the trade, this has variously served as a prison, workhouse, almshouse, wool store and, during World War II, a nursery school, restaurant and home for evacuees. Today it is owned by the National Trust and houses a museum which covers 700 years of the wool trade. **Little Hall** (Easter to October), the lovely ochre, half-timbered building on the market place, is the headquarters of the Suffolk Preservation Society; the house and gardens are open to the public.

Little Hall in Lavenham

Gainsborough in Sudbury

43

Lavenham: Guildhall detail

Colchester Castle

Tour 2

Colchester and Constable Country

Colchester Castle and museums – Dedham – East Bergholt – Flatford Mill – Hadleigh – Kersey *See map on page 40*

The route begins by exploring past civilisations in the Norman keep of Colchester, oldest recorded town in Britain. A short distance away, the countryside around Dedham and East Bergholt was the inspiration of John Constable, arguably the greatest English landscape painter of the 19th century. In spite of changes and tourism, visitors can still savour the peaceful scenes of the Stour Valley, recognisable from Constable's paintings.

The Stour Valley

Colchester owes its rich history to its setting on the River Colne, 8 miles (13km) from the sea. Known as Camulodunum (fortress of the Celtic war god, Camulos), it became the first capital of Roman Britain. In AD60 Queen Boadicea of the Iceni tribe destroyed the town and castle before going on to do likewise in London and St Albans. The Romans rebuilt the town, this time erecting a 10-ft (3-m) thick defensive wall around the city. A long section of this original town wall, the oldest in Britain, and the largest surviving Roman gateway, still stand.

In 1076–1125 William the Conqueror built the Norman castle on the ruins of the Roman Temple of Claudius, using many of the Roman bricks. All that remains of the mighty fortress is the great ★★ **Norman Keep**, the largest in Britain and now home to the ★★ **Castle Museum** (March to November Monday to Saturday 10am–5pm, Sunday 2–5pm; winter Monday to Saturday 10am–5pm).

The closest large car parks, open daily, are in Priory Street (CBC), southeast of the castle, and Osborne Street (NCP), south of the castle.

The wide-ranging collection within the museum charts the history of Colchester from prehistory to the Civil War. The Roman galleries are outstanding, featuring exquisite Roman glass and jewellery, statues, mosaics, military tombstones and, for children, hands-on exhibits, video clips and armour to try on. Displays also cover Norman and medieval Colchester and the siege of the town during the English Civil War.

Castle Museum: Roman exhibits

In the 16th century Flemish weavers settled in Colchester to boost the textile trade. The gabled and timber-framed houses of the peaceful **Dutch quarter** can be seen in Maidenburgh Street, bordering Castle Park behind the castle. Colchester's other attractions are also within easy walking distance of the castle. Just east of the castle entrance, the **Holly Trees Museum** houses a collection of bygones within an elegant Georgian mansion. Across the road from the Visitor Information Centre, the small **Natural History Museum** within All Saints Church concentrates on the local natural environment. The town's two other museums are on Trinity Street, to the west, close to the modern shopping precincts. The **Social History Museum** is housed within Holy Trinity Church, which retains a Saxon tower. **Tymperleys Clock Museum**, a restored 15th-century timber-framed house, has a fascinating collection of locally-crafted, antique timepieces.

45

The Social History Museum

From Colchester follow the signs for the A12 to Ipswich, which you join 2 miles (3km) north of the city. Take the ★ **Dedham** exit and continue to follow the signs to the village. If there are no parking spaces along the main street – often the case is this highly popular village – follow the signs to the car park near the river. The soaring tower of the splendid flint ★ **Church of St Mary**, built in 1492–1520 with profits from the wool trade, features in several of Constable's paintings. Today Dedham is prosperous stockbroker belt territory, and the main street is lined by finely preserved medieval and Georgian houses. The United Reform Church is home to the **Dedham Arts and Crafts Centre**, where visitors can often watch craftsmen at work. **Castle House**, a mile (1.5km) south of the centre, was the home of the horse painter Sir Alfred Munnings, and contains a collection of his works of art.

From Dedham the B1029 takes you past the **Dedham Rare Breeds Farm** (end March to September, 10.30am–5.30pm), and Dedham Mill (converted to residences) on the River Stour. Constable used to walk daily along the river from his home in East Bergholt to the grammar school in Dedham. Visitors can take a rowing boat from here to

Constable's home remembered in East Bergholt

A heavy toll at St Mary's Church

Flatford or follow the 1½-mile (2.5-km) footpath – but motorists must make a much longer, circuitous route of 5½ miles (9km) to reach the mill. Continue along the B1029 and turn left under the A12 at the church of Stratford St Mary. Turn left again, signposted Flatford, to join the A12. The road to East Bergholt (B1070) is marked off the motorway.

Coming into **East Bergholt** bear right at the Carriers Arms pub. The little house beside the garage near the post office was Constable's early studio. Before the church on the left, a **plaque** on the railings marks the site of East Bergholt House, the painter's childhood home. The parish **St Mary's Church** has the graves of Constable's parents and Willy Lot, whose cottage he painted. Inside, a narrow, unremarkable panel at the foot of the first stained glass window on the right commemorates the artist. The **large wooden cage** in the churchyard houses the heaviest bells currently being rung in England. The church bell tower was begun in 1525, but work ceased through lack of funds and the cage was built as a temporary protection for the bells. It has remained in the churchyard ever since and its bells are rung every Sunday.

From the church follow the signs for ★ **Flatford** which will bring you to Flatford Mill car park where a path leads down to the River Stour. From an early age Constable captured his rural homeland on canvas and several of his greatest works of art depict scenes which lay within a few hundred yards of his home. Short guided walks (June to September afternoons) show you the famous scenes which he painted, comparing what you see now to reproductions of the paintings. **Flatford Mill**, best viewed from across the water, and Willy Lott's Cottage (on the near side of the river) are both recognisable as subjects of the famous *Haywain* painted in 1821. The mill, which belonged to Constable's father, is now owned by the National Trust and leased out as a field studies centre. On the same side of the river the Granary Barn Museum houses an idiosyncratic collection of bygones, mainly on an agricultural theme.

Flatford Mill

Rejoin the B1070, which goes northwest to **Hadleigh**. A busy market town in the valley of the River Brett, this was one of the country's most prosperous wool towns in the 14th and 15th centuries. Houses of various architectural styles, including good examples of half-timbering and pargetting, line the High Street. From Hadleigh the first left turning off the northbound A1141 leads to ★ **Kersey**. A timeless village of timbered houses and colour-washed cottages, set on a steep-sided valley and crowned by the flint tower of its church, Kersey oozes with charm and was described by Pevsner as 'the most picturesque village in South Suffolk'.

Tour 3

The Suffolk Heritage Coast

Woodbridge – Orford – Snape – Aldeburgh – Dunwich – Blythburgh – Southwold *See map on page 40*

Pounded by the North Sea, the Suffolk coast has been subject to steady erosion for centuries. In the Middle Ages, entire towns were lost to the sea and the silting up of rivers reduced trading ports to mere villages. One bonus of the erosion (which continues at a metre a year) is the absence of developers. The small coastal towns and villages are delightfully unspoilt and the marshes and mudflats remain a haven for wildlife.

The route starts in **Woodbridge**, an unspoilt market town at the head of the Deben estuary. Downstream from the town, at Sutton Hoo, excavations in 1939 revealed the rotting timbers of an 89-ft (27-m) long ship, thought to have been used as the burial chamber of the Saxon King Raedwald of East Anglia. The treasures, including priceless armoury, silver, gold and jewellery, are on display in the British Museum. Excavations continue at the site.

    In Tudor times Woodbridge was a flourishing centre for shipbuilding, sailmaking and weaving. Large boats can no longer navigate the River Deben, but this is still a favourite spot among the boating fraternity, much of the activity focusing on the busy quayside and yacht harbour. The white clapboard ★ **Tide Mill**, dating from the 18th century, has been restored to working order, and operates according to the tides. Narrow streets lead up from the quay to the town centre, well worth exploring for its Georgian streets, antique shops and galleries and charming Market Hill.

Tide Mill in Woodbridge

From Woodbridge, take the A1152 going east, then turn off at the B1084 signed to **Orford** (11 miles/17.5km from Woodbridge). Once a thriving port and town, this is now a mere village dominated by the mighty keep of the former ★★ **Orford Castle** (daily in summer, 10am–6pm; winter 10am–1pm, 2–4pm) built by Henry II as part of a series of coastal defences in 1165. The gradual formation by the North Sea of the shingle spit (Orford Ness) led to the demise of the port and the decline of what were originally extensive castle fortifications. The 90-ft (27-m) high keep, the oldest five-sided keep in the country, soars above the village, commanding splendid views over the River Alde and Orford Ness.

    On the village square the Butley Orford Oysterage has long been famous for fish and seafood. Just up the road, above a craft shop selling magnificent log baskets,

Local crafts in Orford

Snape Maltings

Aldeburgh's Moot Hall

House in the Clouds

Dunwich Underwater Exploration illustrates the erosion along the coast and displays relics brought up by divers from the lost town of Dunwich (*see page 49*). The nearby medieval church, vast in proportion to today's village, was the setting of some of the early performances by the composer Benjamin Britten. The road past the old Jolly Sailor Inn leads to Orford Quay where local boats or the *Lady Florence* cruiser make trips along Orford Ness to Havergate Island to see avocets and other waders.

At the junction a mile (1.5km) north of Orford, take the unclassified road ahead marked Aldeburgh. In 4 miles (6.5km) the road joins the B1069 at Snape. Formerly known as Snapes, meaning 'boggy place', the village is today known primarily for ★ **Snape Maltings**, the 19th-century complex of red brick granaries and malthouses, converted by Benjamin Britten into a concert hall in 1967. His opera *Peter Grimes*, based on an outcast from George Crabbe's poem *The Borough*, was performed here in 1945. The main Aldeburgh Festival of Music and Arts takes place here in June (Box Office, tel: 01728 453543), but other musical events are held here and throughout the region from Easter to October. Within the Snape complex, riverside galleries and shops, selling crafts, plants and antiques, are open all year.

The B1069 going north from Snape joins the A1094 which runs east to ★ **Aldeburgh**. This unspoilt seaside town resort acquired international fame through the Aldeburgh festival held here until the new premises were acquired at Snape. It is still very much a festival centre, hosting concerts and exhibitions and accommodating Snape audiences in its hotels and restaurants. The High Street of galleries, groceries and book shops runs parallel to a long, steeply-shelving shingle beach where fresh fish is sold straight from the boats. On the seafront the brick and timber-framed Tudor **Moot Hall**, originally well inland from the sea, houses a museum of the town's maritime past.

A narrow coastal road links Aldeburgh to **Thorpeness**, an Edwardian model village and site of a 64-acre (25-hectare) boating lake and the 'House in the Clouds' – a conspicuous water tower with a holiday apartment perched on top. Take the B1353 inland to Aldringham, and turn right on to the B1122 for Leiston. A right turn in the town marks the way to **Sizewell nuclear power station** (tel: 01728 642139, daily 10am–4pm) where the Visitor Centre has an exhibition of energy, nuclear power and the environment. Keep on the B1122 through Leiston; just north of the town are the flint and brick ruins of its 14th-century abbey. Three miles (5km) north of Leiston, turn right on

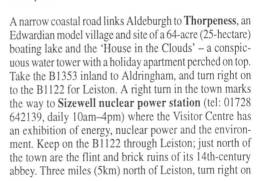

to the B1125 for Westleton. Coming out of the village a right turn takes you along a narrow road to Dunwich. Before reaching the village a road to the right leads to **Dunwich Heath** – a wide expanse of heather and scrubland, commanding splendid views of the unspoilt coastline. The converted coastguard cottages, overlooking the nature reserve at Minsmere, provide an observatory and information centre.

Dunwich itself was formerly the medieval capital of East Anglia, a prosperous town of eight churches, two monasteries, two hospitals, major shipyards and a population half the size of London. Coastal erosion was checked for 200 years by the planting of faggots, but in January 1286 a terrible storm deposited a million tonnes of sand and shingle into the harbour, destroying its status as a port. Further damage was caused by the storm of 1326 and the population plummeted to 600. Constant erosion over the centuries has reduced the village to a handful of houses, a pub, a church and a beach with a café and a few fishing boats.

Leper Chapel in Dunwich

49

All that remains of medieval Dunwich are the ruins of the Grey Friars monastery and those of the **Leper Chapel** by the church. A solitary tombstone is the only testimony to the former presence of the medieval All Saints Church, which fell into the sea in 1921. The sound of the church bells tolling from the sea bed can be heard when a storm is threatening – or so the locals say.

The ★ **Dunwich Museum** (daily March to April 2pm–4.30pm; Easter to September 11.30am–4.30pm; October noon–4pm) charts the history of the town from Roman times to the present day. The most intriguing exhibit is the model of Dunwich in its heyday, showing all the medieval buildings lost to the sea. At the present rate of erosion the museum has 75 years to go.

Strolling on Dunwich Heath

Blythburgh Church

Take the road past the pub and museum, through Dunwich Forest to join the B1125. Turn right for **Blythburgh**, crossing the B1387. The wool trade of this previously prosperous port left its mark in its vast ★ **church** (on the far side of the A12). Rising majestically above the tiny village and seen for miles around, it is known locally as 'the Cathedral of the Marshes'. In a great storm in 1577 the church steeple crashed through the roof, killing three of the congregation. Some claim the visitor was the Devil, who left his scorchmarks on the inside of the great north door. Another unwelcome visitor who left his mark was the Puritan iconoclast, William Dowsing, who as Parliamentary Visitor to the Churches of Suffolk, smashed the windows and statues, fixed tethering rings to the pillars for his horses and left bullets in the timber roof.

Follow the A12 towards ★ **Southwold**, turning right on to the A1095. Thanks to the closure in 1929 of the railway line which linked the town to London, this is a remarkably unspoilt and charmingly old-fashioned resort. Set on a clifftop, and swept by stiff sea breezes, it is distinctive for its open greens, created after a fire destroyed most of the town in 1659.

Beach huts in Southwold

The town retains a variety of architectural styles: Georgian and Regency houses, Victorian seafront terraces, fishermen's cottages, and buildings with a marked Dutch influence, reflecting trade with northern Europe. To the east the sand and shingle beach is backed by colourful bathing huts; to the south sailing and fishing boats are beached by the River Blyth.

The **Southwold Museum** on Bartholomew Green (Easter to September, daily, 2.30– 4.30pm) is devoted to local history with special exhibits on the Southwold railway and the Battle of Sole Bay, fought off the coast in 1672 between the combined British and French fleets against the Dutch. The Victorian Sole Bay Inn, in the shadow of the soaring white lighthouse, lies conveniently close to the famous Adnams brewery, and has its ales supplied by horse-drawn drays. On the seafront the Southwold Sailors' Reading Room is a social club for retired seamen, built in 1864 to deter fishermen from taking to the bottle, fishing on Sundays or other unholy pursuits. The room, full of maritime exhibits, is open to the public.

Southwold's ★ **Church of St Edmund**, one of the few buildings to escape the town fire of 1659, is regarded by many as the finest medieval seaside church in England. Noteable features of the light, spacious interior are the painted rood-screen, the finely carved choir stalls and, on one of the pillars, the little wooden figure known as Southwold Jack, who used to strike the bell to announce the start of services.

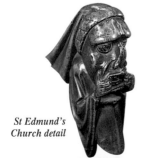

St Edmund's Church detail

Tour 4

Norwich: medieval armour in the castle

Norwich – A City Stroll

Castle – Royal Arcade – Market – Church of St Peter Mancroft – Bridewell Alley – Bridewell Museum – St Andrew's and Blackfriars Hall – Elm Hill – Tombland – Cathedral – Pull's Ferry *See map on page 53*

51

Until the industrial revolution Norwich was one of the most prosperous cities in England. Set amid rich agricultural land it rose to prominence in the Middle Ages as a market and trading centre, growing rich on its trade of worsted cloth. Tradition has it that the city had a pub for each day of the year and a church for every Sunday. Today there is ample evidence of its former prosperity, with 32 medieval churches and a wealth of historic houses. The city also has a large and colourful market, inviting cafés and pubs and a pleasantly relaxed atmosphere.

Norwich is 63 miles (109km) northeast of Cambridge, on the A14 and A11, and 115 miles (184km) northeast of London, on the M11 and A11. The closest car parks to the castle, where the walk starts, are at Castle Mall, the new multi-storey shopping complex. The Level 2 exit at Castle Meadow leads to the path to the castle.

Castle interior

On a mound above the town, the gaunt ★★ **Castle** ❶ (Monday to Saturday 10am–5pm, Sunday 2–5pm) has stood guard over the city for over 900 years. The Norman Keep, which is all that remains of the original edifice, was refaced in 1834 – hence the newer-than-Norman look. In 1220 the castle became the county gaol and remained so for 650 years, until it was bought by the city for conversion to a museum and public park. It is well worth joining one of the guided tours, which take you up to the battlements for splendid views and down to the dungeons for an insight into the grim existence of its inmates. Executions, held outside the castle, drew crowds of spectators and, in the case of the hanging of James Rush for murder in 1848, excursion trains were laid on from London. The Keep interior, albeit changed over the centuries, gives some idea of how the building might have looked when the Normans were garrisoned here.

The Castle Museum, converted from the old prison blocks, houses collections of archaeology from prehistory to the 18th century, natural history, porcelain and paintings. The highlights are the works of art by the Norwich School (1803–33), a group of landscape painters who drew their inspiration from the Norfolk scenery. The leading figures were John Sell Cotman, one of Britain's greatest watercolourists, and John Crome, whose oil paintings were inspired by the Dutch 17th-century landscapists.

Snack time at the market

Leave the castle by the steps going down to Castle Street. Cross the road for the **Royal Arcade ❷**, the elegant art nouveau thoroughfare leading to the market. (This closes out of shopping hours, in which case take the parallel Davey Place to the north.) At the far end of the arcade the **Market ❸**, which has been held here for over 900 years, is a focus of city life. The canopied stalls, selling everything from clothes to fresh cockles and crabs, are tightly packed into the large sloping square. On the far side, overlooking the scene is the huge City Hall (1938); to the right is the flint and stone **Guild Hall ❹**, housing the tourist information centre and a collection of Norwich civic regalia and plate; and to the left looms the tower of the Perpendicular ★ **Church of St Peter Mancroft ❺**. The finest of the city's medieval churches, this has a wonderfully light and lofty interior, with a magnificent hammerbeam roof and notable stained glass in the east window depicting the lives of the saints.

The Mustard Shop

From Exchange Street going north from the market take the first right for Bedford Street. At the corner basket shop turn left for **Bridewell Alley**, one of the oldest shopping streets in the city and home to the **Mustard Shop**. Farmers in East Anglia have been growing mustard for Colman for over 100 years, and this specialist shop-cum-museum sells several varieties, as well as mustard pots and souvenirs. Further along on the right the **Bridewell Museum ❻** (April to September, Tuesday to Saturday 10am–5pm, Sunday 2–5pm) is housed within a former bridewell, or prison for petty criminals. In the 1800s it became a tobacco factory, later a leather warehouse and finally a shoe factory, making it a fitting setting for a museum devoted to local industries and crafts. Exhibits include a chemist shop, Norwich textiles, shoes and clocks.

Bridewell Museum exhibit

Cross St Andrew's Street for **St Andrew's and Black-friars Hall** ❼, which together once formed the Dominican Blackfriars convent church. The lofty interior of St Andrew's Hall, whose walls are hung with portraits of former mayors of Norwich, nowadays makes a fine setting for concerts, craft fairs, the beer festival and other events.

Exiting the Hall, turn left up Princes Street, passing the pretty pink Garsett (or Armada) House said to incorporate wood from ships of the Spanish Armada. Further up the hill the Perpendicular **Church of St Peter Hungate** ❽ (April to September, Monday to Saturday 10am–5pm) is nowadays a museum of ecclesiastical art and a brass rubbing centre. The steeply sloping ★★ **Elm Hill** ❾, saved from demolition by the Norwich Society, is the city's medieval showpiece. Originally the home of wealthy merchants, the narrow cobbled street is flanked by beautifully preserved 16th to 18th-century houses. The house at numbers 22–24, built after a fire in 1507, is particularly fine, with its exposed red brickwork and oak beams. The lower levels of the houses are given over to specialist shops, many selling crafts and antiques. The elm tree which gave the street its name died of Dutch elm disease and has been replaced with a plane tree.

Turn right at the end of Elm Hill, up to **Tombland**, the former Saxon market place. To the right, opposite the entrance to the cathedral, lies the quaint Tombland Alley with the 16th-century half-timbered Stewards House on the corner. To the right of the cathedral entrance is a memorial to Edith Cavell, the Norwich-born nurse who was executed by the Germans for helping prisoners-of-war escape

The Stewards House in Tombland

53

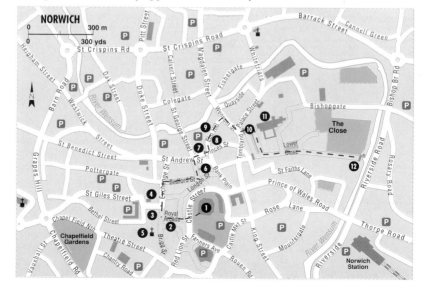

Town crier

NORWICH

*Norwich Cathedral and
a roof boss in the cloisters*

from Belgium during World War I. **Erpingham Gate** ⑩ was built by Sir Thomas Erpingham who led the English archers at Agincourt in 1415 and whose statue occupies a niche over the arch. The gate leads into tranquil Cathedral Close, where some of the houses originated as monastic buildings. Many of the buildings, including the Church of St Ethelbert, were destroyed in 1272 by rioting citizens.

The magnificent ★★ **Cathedral** ⑪ (daily 7.15am–6pm) was founded in 1096 by Bishop Herbert de Losinga, and completed in 1145. The core of flints and mortar came from East Anglia but the pale stone of the exterior was shipped all the way from Caen in Normandy. The sheer size and grandeur of the cathedral is best appreciated from the west end. The massive Norman pillars and the three tiers of arches support the magnificent vaulted roof. The original wooden roof, destroyed by fire, was replaced in the 15th and 16th centuries with stone vaulting and embellished by **carved and painted bosses** illustrating stories from the Bible. There are 1,106 of these throughout the cathedral, of which 225 decorate the nave. Beyond the organ screen, the choir, where the monks worshipped, has elaborate wooden carvings on the canopies and also on the misericords (the shelves on the underside of the tip-up seats) where the medieval scenes depict strife, conquest of evil, sloth, greed and mortal sins. Behind the high altar the treasured fragments of the original bishop's throne – placed here by the Normans – lie below the modern wooden throne. Radiating from the ambulatory are small chapels housing medieval painted panels, the finest of which is the highly coloured and detailed reredos in St Luke's Chapel. The cloisters, which are the largest in England, are entered from the south side of the cathedral. Here the roof bosses can be seen more closely, and the progression in style of the tracery is evidence of the long period of construction (1297–1430).

For exterior views of the Norman apse and the flying buttresses leave the cathedral by the door leading from the south transept. Go straight on for the Lower Close Green where the monastic brew-house and bake-house used to stand. Today it the setting of some very desirable residential properties. On the far corner of the green, a road leads down to Pull's Ferry, the route of the medieval canal dug to transport the Caen Cathedral stone on its last leg. **Pull's Ferry** ⑫, named after an 18th-century ferryman, is a medieval flint and stone watergate on the River Wensum. From here you can admire the spire of the cathedral which is second only to Salisbury in height. From Pull's Ferry return to the centre; alternatively take the Riverside Walk which leads north to the 14th-century Cow Tower, the oldest surviving brick building in Norwich.

Pull's Ferry

Tour 5

The Great Ouse at King's Lynn

North Norfolk Coast

King's Lynn – Castle Rising – Sandringham – Heacham – Hunstanton – The Burnhams – Holkham Hall – Blakeney – Cley – Felbrigg Hall – Cromer – Blickling Hall *See map on page 57*

From historic King's Lynn the route heads north to explore the string of villages along the North Norfolk coast. Designated as an Area of Outstanding Natural Beauty, the marshes, dunes, sand and shingle provide a haven for bird-watchers, boating enthusiasts and ramblers. Combined with the coastal villages and resorts are some of Norfolk's finest country mansions.

Navigation light

The route starts at ★ **King's Lynn**, seaport and market town on the River Great Ouse south of the Wash. An important trading port in the Middle Ages, the town was granted various royal charters, the first of them conferred by King John. Following his last visit to the city, just before he died in 1216, his royal convoy, carrying all the Crown Jewels, miscalculated the tide and disappeared in the Wash. Divers have been searching for the missing treasure ever since.

The riverside warehouses and the ships arriving to berth at the docks and grain silos are evidence that Lynn (as it is commonly called) is still a busy port. The heart of the town has maintained its character, with fine Georgian houses and medieval monuments. Saturday Market Place is overlooked by the twin-towered medieval Church of St Margaret and the 15th-century **Trinity Guildhall**, containing the Regalia Rooms and the Old Gaol House, where audio-visual tours take you through the more gruesome

Customs House

aspects of Lynn's history. Beyond the Purfleet, overlooked by the elegant **Customs House** (1683), King Street is flanked by historic houses and buildings, the most distinguished of which is the Guildhall of St George (1406). At the end of the street, the Tuesday Market Place, occupying three acres, is one of the finest market squares in the country.

From King's Lynn follow the A149 Hunstanton signs. Where the road meets the A148, 4 miles (6.5 km) from King's Lynn, a diversion can be made eastwards to ★★ **Houghton Hall** (Easter to September, Sunday, Thursday and Bank Holiday Monday 2–5.30pm), the grand Palladian house built in 1722–35 by Britain's first Prime Minister, Sir Robert Walpole.

On the A149, 5 miles (8km) north of King's Lynn, a sign to the left marks ★ **Castle Rising**, a fine example of a Norman keep. In another 2 miles (3km) a left turning marked Wolferton takes you to the ★ **Wolferton Station Museum**, the former royal retiring rooms built for King Edward VII and Queen Alexandra in 1898. This houses a fascinating collection of royal, railway-related memorabilia including Queen Victoria's travelling bed.

Sandringham

Back on the A149 the next turning right leads to the ★ **Sandringham** estate (Easter to early October, except last week of July and first week of August, daily 11.00am–4.45pm). Bought in 1862 by Queen Victoria and Prince Albert for the Prince of Wales (later Edward VII), the estate passed down through four generations of monarchs and is now the country retreat of the Queen. Provided she is not in residence, the house, museum and gardens, comprising 60 acres (24 hectares) of splendid grounds with lakes and walks, are open to the public.

The beach resorts start at Snettisham and from here the A149 can become clogged with summer traffic. At **Heacham**, north of Snettisham, the Caley Mill lavender fields provide a blaze of colour from mid-June to mid-August. Guided tours take place in the summer months but the plant centre and gift shop are open all year.

Two miles (3km) north of Heacham, **Hunstanton** (or 'Hunston' as the locals call it) is the only East Anglian resort facing west, and as such enjoys some glorious sunsets over the Wash. It was here that St Edmund, King of East Anglia, is said to have landed in 850AD, the ruins of St Edmund's Chapel marking the spot. Today it is a popular holiday resort, with broad sandy beaches and 60-ft (18-m) cliffs distinctive for their coloured stripes of carrstone and red and white chalk. On the promenade the **Sealife Centre** (tel: 01485 533576, open all year) has an underwater tunnel which provides exciting close en-

Sealife Centre resident

counters with numerous species of marine life, from shrimps to sharks.

Beyond Hunstanton the A149 follows the coast eastwards through a series of small villages. Between Brancaster Staithe and Holkham there are seven 'Burnham' villages, three of them now merging as Burnham Market. The most westerly is **Burnham Deepdale**, which has a church with a round Saxon tower and a Norman font with carved panels of farming scenes depicting each month of the year. **Burnham Market**, the showpiece village, signed off to the right just after Burnham Norton, has a wide green and handsome Georgian houses. **Burnham Thorpe**, reached by taking the first turn left off the Fakenham road from Burnham Market, is famous as the birthplace of Nelson (1758–1805). The 13th-century All Saints' Church, which flies the White Ensign, is full of Nelson memorabilia, including the cross and lectern which are constructed from HMS Victory timbers.

Burnham Deepdale: glass in the church

England's great Admiral may well have taken his first sailing lesson at **Burnham Overy Staithe** before he went to sea at the age of 12. The village was established when the River Burn silted up and boats could no longer reach the seaport, at what is now Burnham Overy Town. It is still a sailing centre, and the harbour in the creek is the starting point for 3-hour boat trips to the nature reserve of Scolt Head island.

57

Holkham, the next village on the A149, is home to one of Norfolk's finest stately homes: ★★ **Holkham Hall** (end May to end September, Sunday to Thursday 1–5pm, plus Easter, spring and summer Bank Holidays on Sunday and Monday 11.30am–5pm; gardens daily 10am–5pm). Set within magnificent parkland, the sombre Palladian facade belies a grandiose hall and state room with paintings by Van Dyck, Gainsborough and Rubens. Within the grounds are the Bygones Museum, featuring agricultural equip-

Holkham Hall

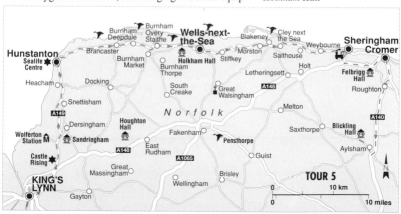

ment, vintage engines and cars, the Holkham Pottery, where craftsmen can often be seen at work, the garden centre within a delightful 19th-century walled garden, a gift shop and gallery.

The park with lake has free entry and makes a delightful spot for picnics.

Wells-next-the-Sea

East of Holkham lies **Wells-next-the-Sea**, a genuine working port, with coasters along the quay and fishing boats bringing in whelks, crabs and shrimps. It is also a popular holiday spot, with a huge caravan site on the dunes behind the beach and an abundance of fast food outlets and amusements by the quay.

The A149 passes through the pretty village of Stiffkey (pronounced 'Stewkey'), famous for 'Stewkey blues' or cockles. Four miles (6.5km) further on ★ **Blakeney** is a pretty coastal village of flint-cobbled cottages, best known for its sand and shingle spit starting at Cley-next-the-Sea in the east and running west beyond Morston. Blakeney Point at its tip is the summer home for about a dozen species of seabirds, including terns, oystercatchers, plovers and redshank. It is also home to common and grey seals, which bask on the sands when the tide is low. From Easter to October these can be spotted on ferry trips which leave from Morston Quay.

Blakeney mariner

East of Blakeney, **Cley-next-the-Sea** (pronounced 'Cly' and no longer next to the sea) became the first Wildlife Trust nature reserve in 1926. The combination of salt marshes, reed beds and lagoons attract a remarkable number of waders, details of which are on display in the Visitors Information Centre. The main landmark of the village is the 18th-century Cley Windmill (Whitsun to September), which has been converted into an attractive guest house.

Cley-next-the-Sea: the windmill

Follow the A149 through Salthouse and Weybourne, where the **Muckleburgh Collection** (mid-February to October, daily 10am–5pm) displays military tanks, armoured vehicles, guns and missiles. East of Weybourne the seaside resort of **Sheringham** was a small fishing village before the North Norfolk Railway was established in the latter part of the 19th century. Today ★ **steam and diesel locomotives** run to the small Georgian town of Holt, providing fine views of sea and wooded heathland.

From Sheringham to Cromer the alternative to the coastal A149, where caravan sites spoil the cliff scenery, is the A148, reached by taking the A1082 south from Sheringham. Less than 2 miles (3km) before Cromer the B1436 going off to the right leads to the 17th-century ★ **Felbrigg Hall** (Easter to October, Monday, Wednesday, Thursday and weekends 1–5pm; gardens 11am–5pm), filled with 18th-century furnishings and paintings collected on the

Grand Tour. The grounds occupy 1,750 acres (700 hectares), with walks through woodland and historic parkland with church and lake.

Clifftop **Cromer** is a pleasantly old-fashioned seaside resort with a long sand and shingle beach and a town centre dominated by the soaring tower of its church. The resort expanded with the advent of the railway and still retains some of its Victorian hotels, as well as a fishing fleet and a pier whose Pavilion Theatre still packs in audiences. The boats bring in fresh fish, lobster and the justly famous Cromer crabs, which are sold throughout Norfolk from Easter to October.

Cromer pier

The route ends at ★★★ **Blickling Hall** (Easter to October, Tuesday, Wednesday, Friday, Saturday, Sunday and Bank Holiday Monday 12.30–4.30pm), regarded by some as the finest Jacobean house in England. Take the A149 south from Cromer, turning off on to the A140, signed Norwich, after 2 miles (3km). The Hall (10 miles/16km south of Cromer) is well signed from the A140.

The red-brick mansion, crowned by turrets, chimneys and gables, and bordered by lawns and huge yew hedges, creates an unforgettable impression. Built by Sir Henry Hobart, it was left to the National Trust by the Marquis of Lothian, ambassador to the US in the early years of World War II and a leading light in the formation of the Trust's country houses scheme. Inside, the state rooms are decorated with richly moulded ceilings and the walls are hung with formal portraits and tapestries. The most remarkable room is the 127-ft (38-m) Long Gallery, built for socialising and indoor exercise but turned into a library in 1745. The grounds consist of classically 18th-century gardens, a lake, and park and woodland offering several miles of footpaths and bridle paths.

59

Blickling Hall and its library

Architecture

Opposite: Peterhouse Chapel

Cambridge

The city's architecture spans almost 1,000 years, from the Saxon tower of St Bene't's Church to the 'high tech' structures of the Science Park. From the 13th century the city's drive towards academic pre-eminence led inevitably to a city dominated by colleges and university, its buildings reflecting the elite architectural aspirations of England as a whole.

The Romans were the first to establish a stronghold here, but there is no visible record of their occupation. The Normans, however, left their mark in the mound of the castle, the Round Church and the remains of the nunnery of St Radegund which formed the nucleus of Jesus College.

The early Gothic period saw a huge and significant spate of building. The first college, Peterhouse, was founded in 1286, giving rise to another seven colleges in the following century. In their early days most of these colleges were relatively simple academic halls, set up specifically for fellows to teach divinity or law to small groups of scholars. In due course they developed into wealthy and complex institutions, with a whole range of facilities for work, rest and worship. The buildings were constructed around an open space, traditionally called a Court (as opposed to Oxford's Quad) and consisting typically of the communal dining hall, the Master's Lodge, student accommodation, a library and – of paramount importance for medieval collegiate life – a chapel. Old Court at Corpus Christi College, and Cloister and Old Courts in Queens', provide superb intact examples of these medieval courts. The character of many others has been substantially altered by the 18th-century fashion of stone facing (ashlaring) over the original clunch or brickwork.

English Gothic reached its climax with King's College Chapel, one of the finest late medieval buildings in Europe. Henry VI demolished a great swathe of the medieval town centre, including wharves, a church and a monastery, to make way for his great foundation. The first overall impression of the chapel is one of homogeneity, but it was in fact constructed over three distinct periods spanning 80 years. Since the local clunch (a soft limestone) was unsuitable for the exterior, a more durable stone was shipped from the college's own quarries in Tadcaster, Yorkshire. On the external walls this white limestone is distinguishable from the buff-coloured oolitic limestone from Northamptonshire and Rutland with which the chapel was completed. The interior decoration reveals a progression of style culminating in Italian Renaissance influence, best seen in the detail on the wooden screen and the stained glass windows financed by Henry VIII.

The Norman Round Church

61

King's College Chapel: exterior detail

The late 15th century and first half of the 16th century gave rise to some of the city's finest colleges: Jesus, Christ's, St John's, Magdalene and Trinity. The ostentatious battlemented gateways of most of these colleges epitomise the movement. The pinnacle of the genre is the grandiose Trinity Great Court, two pre-existing courts knocked into one under Henry VIII's grand scheme to create an integrated academic environment unsurpassed anywhere before or since.

The latter half of the 17th century was characterised by a shift towards Renaissance-inspired classical architecture. The first complete Renaissance building was Pembroke College Chapel (1663–65), designed by Sir Christopher Wren. A number of local architects, including James Essex and James Burrough, made important contributions to the era, but the outstanding classical work of the city is indisputably Wren's library at Trinity – an immaculately proportioned and restrained rectangular edifice, raised on pillars above a cloister.

St John's College: New Court

The 19th century was an era of astonishing architectural expansion. The revivalist fashion of the 1830s gave birth to William Wilkin's main court at Downing, his New Court at St John's and the Gatehouse and Screen at King's. Under the Victorians many new sites sprouted to meet the needs of the increased number of students and subjects. In some cases older buildings were demolished or subjected to heavy-handed restoration.

Concrete at Queens' College

The 20th century has seen the city fairly and squarely within the mainstream of international design. By the 1930s local architecture was feeling the influence of the International Modern Movement, inspired by the aggressive, innovate style of Le Corbusier. The exposed brick and concrete blocks of the 1950s and 60s, such as Queens' Erasmus Building on the Backs, sparked inevitable controversy. The most controversial of all was Sir James Stirling's prize-winning History Faculty, an unrestrained glass-faced structure of the 1960s, which became notorious for its leaking roof, collapsing tile cladding and problems of ventilation. One of the most successful buildings of the era was the Cripps Building of St John's.

Buildings of the last three decades have seen a shift from the brutal to the vernacular. In the case of the late 1970s Robinson College, the exterior clad in hand-made bricks and tiling, looks back to medieval castle architecture. Some of the city's most adventurous new buildings form part of the burgeoning business parks. The boldest and most exciting industrial constructions have been the Napp Laboratories on the Science Park, the spider-like Schlumberger building on Madingley Road and the energy-efficient Ionica building on the St John's Innovation Park.

Emphasis on natural light and ecological management

Saffron Walden's Town Hall

is evident in many exciting new buildings, including Norman Foster's University Law Faculty, a vast, light-filled pavilion fashioned in stainless steel and silicon glazing; Fitzwilliam College Chapel, a simple, elegant structure with the imagery of a ship; and Jesus College library, whose brickwork exterior blends with its Tudor surrounds.

63

East Anglia

Norwich: Church of St Peter Mancroft

The great medieval churches which are so much part of the East Anglian landscape were built in the 14th and 15th centuries, when the cloth and weaving industries made East Anglia the wealthiest and most densely populated region of England. In villages and towns, regardless of the size of the population, affluent merchants vied to build the biggest and grandest churches.

Many of the monuments suffered both under Reformist destruction and Victorian heavy-handed restoration, but in general they are remarkably well preserved. Characteristic features are the flint flushwork walls, the light, spacious interiors and the fine woodwork, especially the timber roofs.

The lack of suitable building stone led to the widespread use of timber and East Anglia has a wealth of beautifully preserved, half-timbered Tudor houses. The best examples can be found in the wool villages and towns of Suffolk *(see Tour 1)*. Lavenham has over 300 examples, the most splendid of which is the Guildhall.

Many of the old house facades were plastered over in the 17th century, some of them embellished with 'pargetting'. This was an ornamental type of plasterwork, with frequent use of the *fleur de lys*, an emblem of the wool trade, and the mitre of St Blaise, patron saint of the wool trade. With the decline of the trade, there were insufficient funds for rebuilding or renovating – hence the abundance of unspoilt buildings enjoyed by later generations.

The Ancient House in Clare with pargetting

The Arts

The distinctive East Anglian landscape was the inspiration for some of Britain's best known artists. John Constable drew inspiration from Suffolk's Stour Valley; Gainsborough, in his *Portrait of Mr and Mrs Andrews*, which has been described as the most English of English pictures, set his subjects in a typical Suffolk landscape; and the Norwich School of Painters, active in the first half of the 19th century, drew common inspiration from the surrounding Norfolk land and seascapes. More recently, Benjamin Britten initiated the Aldeburgh Festival and turned the area into a centre of musical activity.

Cambridge is linked with a large number of leading literary figures, including Milton, Wordsworth, Byron, Tennyson, Pepys and Coleridge. In the years before World War I, the rural retreat of Grantchester formed the backdrop to a group of leading lights, among them the poet Rupert Brooke and the writers Virginia Woolf and E.M. Forster. Beyond Cambridge, at Bury St Edmunds, Charles Dickens gave readings in the Assembly Rooms and immortalised the Angel Hotel in *The Pickwick Papers*.

Gainsborough House in Sudbury

Music and Theatre

Concert in St Mary's Church

Cambridge offers a wide range of musical events. Classical concerts are performed in college chapels, in the University West Road Concert Hall (tel: 01223 335182) and in The Corn Exchange (tel: 01223 357851), which also hosts ballet, pop and rock concerts and touring theatre groups. During the summer, classical and contemporary music festivals are held in various venues around the city.

The Cambridge Arts Theatre, one of the most innovative venues of drama, dance, opera and comedy in the country, has been the launch-pad of some famous names: Fonteyn danced *Swan Lake* here, Britten conducted *The Turn of the Screw* and Pinter premiered *The Birthday Party*. The ADC Theatre, Park Street (tel: 01223 352001) is home to the University Dramatic Club; the Mumford Theatre (tel: 01223 352932) hosts theatre, music and dance, mainly by local amateurs; while the Cambridge Drama Centre (tel: 01223 322748) off Mill Road offers a wide range of plays and workshops. During the Shakespeare Festival (July to October) open-air productions take place in college gardens. The Junction (tel: 01223 511511) is the city's main theatre venue for the young.

Major venues for music in East Anglia are Snape Maltings, home of the Aldeburgh Festival, the cathedrals of Ely and Peterborough, the Theatre Royal and the Cathedral in Bury St Edmunds, and the Corn Exchange in King's Lynn. Norwich's Theatre Royal hosts major touring productions of opera, ballet and drama.

Shakespeare in the open air

Calendar of Events

Show time

Details of various events can be obtained from the Tourist Information offices listed on page 75.

May
Ascension Day – St John's College Choir sings hymns from the top of the college tower. **Bury St Edmunds Festival** – 17 days of concerts and theatre.

June
Midsummer Fair, Midsummer Common, Cambridge. **Cambridge University 'May' Bumps** – college crews race on the river. **'May Week'** – 'May Balls' and other college events. **Honorary degree ceremony**, Senate House, Cambridge. **Aldeburgh Festival of Music and Arts**, Snape Maltings, Suffolk (*see page 48*).

Going to the Ball

July
'Summer in the City' with fireworks, Parker's Piece, Cambridge. **Cambridge Film Festival**. **Cambridge Folk Festival**. **City Bumps** – town crews compete for the head of the river. **King's Lynn Festival of Arts and Music** – held for 9 days towards the end of the month.

October
Norfolk and Norwich Festival – music, theatre, opera and literature at venues in both town and country.

November
Guy Fawkes Night – fireworks, bonfire and fair on Midsummer Common.

December
Festival of lessons and carols in King's College Chapel.

Food and Drink

Opposite: traditional fudge making near King's College

Cambridge has a surprising paucity of good places to eat. Restaurants come and go with alarming rapidity and for the last few years the only consistently good restaurant for the discerning customer has been Twenty-Two (*see below*). The other success story is Browns, not for gastronomy, but for reliable plain and affordable food, appealing to all ages. There is also a wide range of ethnic restaurants, particularly Chinese, Indian, Greek and Thai. Cambridge has no specialities of its own but the food shopping scene is thriving. The market is excellent for fresh fish, cheese, teas and coffee beans, and the town has several high-quality delicatessens and health-food shops.

Seafood in abundance

East Anglia is well known for its **seafood**. Cromer is famous for its crabs, Wells for whelks, Colchester for oysters. Norfolk is also known for turkeys, samphire ('poor man's asparagus') and **mustard**, which has been made here since 1814. (For the Norwich mustard shop, *see page 52*.) Suffolk, which used to ship malt to breweries in London and Norwich, has three **local breweries**. Tolly Cobbold in Ipswich and Greene King in Bury St Edmunds both welcome visitors to see the brewing of real ale, using traditional techniques. Adnams in Southwold still delivers its ale to surrounding pubs by horse and cart.

67

The region also offers plenty of opportunities to taste **cider, apple juice and wine**. A number of vineyards produce their own wines and offer tours or walks and wine tasting: Carters' Vineyards, Green Lane, Boxted, Essex, tel: 01206 271136; Shawgate Vineyard, Badingham Road, Framlingham, Suffolk, tel: 01728 724060; and Bruisyard Vineyard and Herb Centre, Church Road, Bruisyard, Suffolk, tel: 01728 638281, producers of the award-winning Bruisyard St Peter wine.

Bruisyard St Peter wine

Restaurant selection
£££ Expensive (over £60 for two); ££ Moderate (£35–60 for two); £ Inexpensive (under £35 for two). Price brackets include house wine.

Cambridge
Twenty-Two, 22 Chesterton Road, tel: 01223 351880. Small, elegant restaurant, converted from a Victorian house north of the city centre near Jesus Green. Imaginative set menus which change monthly. Stylish cuisine, beautifully presented. Open for dinner only. £££
Browns, 23 Trumpington Street, tel: 01223 461655. Spacious, lively brasserie, with potted plants, polished floors, fans, mirrors and papers to read. Open all day, every day for breakfast, lunch, tea, dinner. Reliable, plain food (leg

Brown's

The Sala Thong for Thai food

of lamb with rosemary, steak, fish pie, pasta, hot sandwiches, huge salads). Caters for all ages (high chairs and cocktails). No booking, hence occasional long waits at weekends. ££

Shao Tao, 72 Regent Street, tel: 01223 353942. Chinese restaurant, specialising in Peking, Szechuan and Hunan cuisine. ££

Hobbs Pavilion, Park Terrace, tel: 01223 367480. Crêperie, with a multitude of sweet and savoury fillings, in the cricket pavilion on Parker's Piece. £

King's Pantry, King's Parade. Popular student haunt for high quality vegetarian food, all dishes cooked fresh on the premises daily. Vegan organic wines. £

Sala Thong, 35 Newnham Road, tel: 01223 323178. Tiny restaurant, very popular for its Thai food. Booking advisable. £

The rest of East Anglia

Melbourn, Cambridgeshire

Pink Geranium, Station Road, Melbourn, near Royston, tel: 01763 260215. 16th-century thatched cottage, with pretty pink dining room, serving some of the best food in the Cambridge area. £££

Ely, Cambridgeshire

Old Fire Engine, 25 St Mary's Street, tel: 01353 662582. Close to the cathedral, in elegant 17th-century building which was formerly the fire engine house. Wholesome British cooking. Bar with open fire, art gallery. ££

Mortimer's in Bury St Edmunds

Bury St Edmunds, Suffolk

Mortimer's, 31 Churchgate Street, tel: 01284 760623. Very popular fish restaurant named after the 19th-century artist, Thomas Mortimer, whose watercolours hang in the dining room. ££

Colchester, Essex

Warehouse Brasserie, Chapel Street, tel: 01206 765656. A chapel converted into an informal bistro, in the centre of town. Particularly good for fish. ££

Le Talbooth on the River Stour

Dedham, Essex

Le Talbooth, Gunhill, off the A12, tel: 01206 323027. Luxurious restaurant in a half-timbered house on the banks of the River Stour. *Alfresco* meals in summer. £££

Harwich, Essex

The Pier, The Quay, tel: 01255 241212. Renowned for seafood, much of it caught locally. Cheaper dishes, including fish and chips, downstairs, *à la carte* in the smarter harbour-view restaurant upstairs. ££

Norwich, Norfolk
Adlard's, 79 Upper St Giles Street, tel: 01603 633522. Highly imaginative French/British cuisine and an award-winning wine list. £££

The Mill in Cambridge

Orford, Suffolk
Butley-Orford Oysterage, Market Hill, tel: 01394 450277. Café/restaurant in coastal village, famous for oysters and other fish and seafood. ££

Cambridge city pubs

Serious beer drinkers should head for the **Salisbury Arms** on Tenison road which has a dozen different real ales. The city's oldest pub, and probably the most popular, is the **Eagle** in Bene't Street in the town centre, a 16th-century coaching inn still retaining its courtyard. The **Free Press**, on Prospect Row, is a tiny, friendly Victorian pub with imaginative, home-made food. The city has several riverside pubs, among them the Tudor **Fort St George** on Midsummer Common and the **Spade and Becket** on Thompson's Lane.

Outside at the Eagle

Cambridge country pubs

Close to Cambridge, the **Green Man**, **Red Lion** and **Rupert Brooke** pubs in the popular village of Grantchester are assured a steady influx of students, locals and tourists. The **Three Horseshoes** at Madingley is a smart thatched inn, highly sought-after for pub and restaurant meals. The idiosyncratic **Tickell Arms** in Whittlesford (dark blue walls, antiques, opera music) has a lovely conservatory and a wide range of food including smoked meats, game casseroles and pies. In Horningsea the **Plough and Fleece** is a village inn with oak beams, open fireplace and traditional home cooking. The **Olde Ferry Boat** at Holywell, overlooking the Great Ouse, provides a wide range of food.

The Green Man in Grantchester

Shopping

King's Parade

The centre of Cambridge is closed to cars from 10am–4pm Monday to Saturday, which makes for pleasant strolling and shopping. The heart of the city is the market square where stalls under striped canvas sell fresh fruit and vegetables, flowers, fish, fabrics, books, clothes and antiques. To the west lies **King's Parade**, bordered on one side by King's College, on the other by bookshops, boutiques, galleries and cafés. At the near end are the university outfitters, Ryder and Amies; further along Troon's has elegant designer wear for women; while just past the National Trust shop, Primavera displays an imaginative range of jewellery, ceramics, glass and metalwork. North of the market square **Rose Crescent** is a pedestrianised street of small exclusive boutiques. To the southeast of the market the uninspiring **Petty Cury** and **Lion Yard** modern shopping precincts sell mainstream clothes, shoes and jewellery. The department stores of the centre, Robert Sayle (a branch of John Lewis), Marks and Spencers, Boots and Woolworths, are located on the main thoroughfare cutting through the town centre, comprising St Andrew's Street and Sidney Street.

The other main area for shopping is the **Grafton Centre** to the east of the centre. This is a modern covered precinct with large department stores (C&A, Debenham's, British Home Stores), a ten-screen cinema, cafés and a wide range of shops open seven days a week.

One of many specialist bookshops

Unsurprisingly, Cambridge has a large number of **bookshops**. Heffers has the lion's share with its main shop in Trinity Street and five other branches selling books. Dillons and Waterstone's have branches in Sidney Street and Bridge Street respectively, and Cambridge University Press Book Shop in Trinity Street sells the works of the oldest printing house in the country. Among the many antiquarian and secondhand bookshops are David's in St Edwards Passage, Heffers' Deighton Bell in Trinity Street, and Galloway and Porter in Green Street and Sidney Street.

Elsewhere in East Anglia, **Norwich** is the best shopping centre combining a wide range of modern shops, including the new Castle Mall complex, a large daily market and appealing specialist shops in the small roads and alleys. East Anglian **craft centres**, where potters, wood turners, glassmakers and other artists can be seen at work, are found in Dedham in Essex, and Wroxham Barns, Banham and Taverham, all in Norfolk. **Potteries** worth a visit are Sutton Windmill Pottery at Sutton, 17 miles (27km) northeast of Norwich, where Malcolm Flatman designs a large range of stoneware pottery and tableware; and The Posting House Pottery in Long Melford, which has an attractive range of practical and elegant pottery.

Active Pursuits

East Anglia offers plenty of opportunities for the actively inclined, both on the coast and inland.

Boating

Miles of quiet waterways provide endless opportunities for boating and canal-cruising. The Norfolk Broads, between Norwich and the coast, offer 200 miles (320km) of navigable waterways, mainly on rivers. Most boats hired out are motor cruisers – information from the Broads Authority, 18 Colegate, Norwich, tel: 01603 610734. Broads Tours at Wroxham, tel: 01603 782207, offer all-weather trips on the Broads; also cruiser line and self-drive day boats from April to November. Boats can also be hired by the hour or day. The rivers of the Fens also provide miles of navigable waterways (tel: 01353 662062).

Narrow boats on the Cam

Coastal estuaries provide superb sailing, as well as organised boat trips in the season. Day trips along the Suffolk coast are organised by the Yacht Station, Oulton Broad, Lowestoft, tel: 01520 513087.

Watersports in Suffolk

Walking

Information on walks is available from visitor centres and tourist information offices. Favourite areas are the Norfolk and Suffolk coasts, the Norfolk Broads, the Stour Valley (the scenes which inspired Constable) and the Thetford Forest. The Peddars Way and Norfolk Coast Path (from Thetford up to the Norfolk coast, then east to Cromer) offers 93 miles (149 km) of easy walking.

Cycling

Cycling along the quieter rural roads of East Anglia can be a delightful way of experiencing the countryside. There are also designated cycle routes throughout the region. Grafham Water, near Huntingdon, has a circular ride of 13 miles (21km) around the reservoir. Thetford Forest offers miles of cycle paths through forest and heathland. Bikes can be hired at both these locations as well as many shops and visitor centres throughout the area.

Birdwatching

Wicken Fen, near Soham, Cambs is the last remaining undrained fen and has waterfowl in winter and breeding marsh birds in summer. Ouse Washes, near Manea, Cambs, is an important inland site for wintering ducks and swans, and breeding black-tailed godwits. On the Norfolk coast, Blakeney Point National Nature Reserve, Cley Marshes, Holme Bird Observatory Reserve and Titchwell Marsh are all havens for birdwatchers. Minsmere in Suffolk, famous for avocets, has a visitor centre, nature trails and hides.

Getting There

By car

Cambridge is linked to London by the M11, the A10 or the A505 combined with the A1. The journey time is 1 hour 15 minutes to 2 hours depending on the route and the traffic in London. The city is well served by the A14 which runs from Felixstowe on the Suffolk coast to the Midlands, where it joins the M6. There are good road links with the Norfolk and Suffolk coasts, including the ferry port of Harwich. The journey time by car from Cambridge to Norwich is between 75 and 90 minutes, to King's Lynn one hour, and to Bury St Edmunds half an hour.

By bus

The National Express coach network (tel: 01223 460711) operates services between Cambridge and many main towns and cities. Their Express Shuttle from Victoria Coach Station, London, departs 17 times a day and takes 1 hour 15 minutes. Cambridge Coach Services (tel: 01223 236333) links Cambridge to Luton, Heathrow and Gatwick airports, with services every hour.

By train

Anglia Railways operate InterCity services between Cambridge and London, with local connecting services within East Anglia. A regular service links Cambridge to London, King's Cross (51 minutes, express service) and Liverpool Street (about one hour, express service). Trains depart every half an hour during the morning and early evening, every hour for the rest of the day. A direct hourly train service connects Stansted airport with Cambridge, taking approximately one hour. Norwich is connected to London Liverpool Street by a regular rail service, average time 1 hour 50 minutes. For general rail information, tel: 0345 484950 (24-hour service).

Shuttle bus in Cambridge 73

By plane

The nearest major airport to Cambridge is Stansted, London's third international airport with many direct flights to and from European cities (airport information, tel: 01279 680500). The airport is 30 miles (48km) from Cambridge, reached in just over half an hour on the M11, by car or coach. Heathrow Airport is 71 miles (113km), Gatwick 95 miles (152km), both linked to Cambridge by a regular coach service. Cambridge Airport (tel: 01223 373737) operates flights to and from Amsterdam with Suckling Airways (tel: 01223 292525). Norwich has a major regional airport (tel: 01603 411923) with international connections via Manchester, Paris or Amsterdam. London Stansted is 65 miles (104km) by road from Norwich.

The home of Suckling Airlines

Getting Around

Cambridge is best seen on foot. Alternatively bikes can be hired but cycling is prohibited in some streets from 10am to 4pm Monday to Saturday and bikes cannot be taken through the colleges. Within East Anglia, National Express coaches and Anglia Railways operate local services, but to explore the countryside, a car is essential.

Bike hire
Bikes can be hired from Geoff's Bike Hire, 65 Devonshire Road, Cambridge, tel: 01223 365629 (near the Railway Station), and from Mike's Bikes, 28 Mill Road, Cambridge, tel: 01223 312591.

Bus
Cambridge Bus Station is in Drummer Street in the centre of the city. Stagecoach Cambus provide services around the city and to the outlying villages. Buses leave every few minutes for the railway station, the journey taking about 7 minutes. An experimental free bus service operates around the town every ten minutes during the daytime. For information on all local buses, contact the Premier Travel Agency at the Bus Station, or contact Cambus by phone, tel: 01223 572300.

For bus service information in Norfolk, tel: 0500 626116, Suffolk 01473 265676, and Essex 0345 000333.

Parking in Cambridge
The centre of Cambridge is closed to traffic from Monday to Saturday 10am–4pm, and there is very little parking other than the multi-storey car parks. These are located at Lion Yard (with access to the Lion Yard shopping centre), Park Street, Gonville Place and the Grafton Centre. Park and Ride schemes operate from Monday to Saturday: from Madingley Road, west of the centre, off Junction 13 of the M11; from Cowley Road, north of the city; and from Clifton Road south of the city. The Park and Ride bus services run into the city centre every 15–30 minutes depending on the time of day.

Boat hire
Punts are available from March to the end of October, weather permitting. For information, contact Scudamore's Boat Yard, Granta Place, near the Mill Pond (tel: 01223 359750). For the Backs, punts can be hired from the Quayside, Bridge Street, or the Mill Pond. For the meadows and Grantchester, punts and rowing boats should be hired from Scudamore's Boat Yard. Boats are charged by the hour and a hefty deposit (or credit card) is required. Chauffeured punts are also available.

Facts for the Visitor

Cambridge Tourist Information Centre

Tourist Information

The Cambridge Tourist Information Centre in Wheeler Street has a wealth of information on the city and surrounding area, including a shop selling guide books. The centre will reserve accommodation for a fee and organise guided tours. Open April to October Monday to Saturday 9am–6pm (from 9.30am Wednesday, to 7pm in high season), Sunday 10.30am– 3.30pm; November to March Monday to Saturday 9am–5.30pm (9.30am Wednesday), closed Sunday; tel: 01223 322640, fax: 01223 463385.

75

Tourist Offices in East Anglia

Bury St Edmunds, tel: 01284 764667
Colchester, tel: 01206 282920
Ely, tel: 01353 662062
Ipswich, tel: 01473 258070
King's Lynn, tel: 01553 763044
Newmarket, tel: 01638 667200
Norwich, tel: 01603 666071
Southwold, tel: 01502 724729

Sightseeing near King's Parade

Cash dispensers and Link machines, Cambridge

Abbey National: St Andrew's Street
Barclays: Bene't Street and Sidney Street
Lloyds: Sidney Street and Regent Street
Midland: Market Hill and St Andrew's Street
National Westminster: Bene't Street and Trinity Street
Royal Bank of Scotland: Hills Road
TSB: St Andrew's Street and Mill Road

Travel services

American Express Travel Service, 25 Sidney Street, tel: 01223 351636.

Guide Friday in Cambridge

Sightseeing tours

Official guided walking tours leave the Tourist Information Centre daily throughout the year and up to five times a day in summer. The two-hour tours include colleges, the historic city, the 'Backs' and King's College Chapel when possible. On summer evenings 'Drama Tours' are organised using characters in costume to bring to life the history of the city. For information, tel: 01223 322640.

Open-top, double-decker bus tours take in some of the colleges, the Backs and the American Cemetery at Madingley (*see page 36*). A ticket is valid all day and passengers can get on and off at their leisure. Tickets are available from: the Guide Friday Tourism Centre at the Railway Station, tel: 01223-362444; Cambridge Classic Tour, tel: 01487 740241; or the main Tourist Information Centre, tel: 01223 322640.

Opening times

The Fitzwilliam Museum closes on Monday, except on Bank Holidays, but most of the university museums close on Sunday. College openings vary considerably, the only consistency being that they all close for the summer revision and examination period from May to mid-June. The majority of colleges are open for at least part of the day during the rest of the year. Some of the best known colleges have an admission charge during the spring and summer. For King's College Chapel openings, *see page 17*. The Tourist Information Centre (*see page 75*) can give up-to-date information on all college opening hours.

In rural East Anglia many of the attractions such as historic houses are closed from November to March. Norwich and Ely cathedrals are open daily throughout the year.

Emergencies

Police, ambulance, fire brigade, tel: 999. Addenbrooke's Hospital, Hills Road, Cambridge, tel: 01223 217118 (Accident and Emergency), 245151 (General Enquiries).

Disabled access

The Tourist Information Centre publishes a guide to Cambridge for the disabled, detailing colleges, churches, museums, shops, and other locations accessible to wheelchairs. Their accommodation brochure contains information on hotels which cater for the disabled. A Shop-mobility Scheme, providing wheelchairs, operates in the Lion Yard and Grafton Centre East car parks.

Postal services

The main post office in Cambridge is in St Andrew's Street, open Monday to Friday 9am–5.30pm, Saturday 9am–7pm, tel: 01223 323325.

Post haste

For Children

Candlemaking at Dedham

In Cambridge children can enjoy the sights from a punt on the River Cam or from the open top of a double-decker bus. Some of the rarely visited university museums have fascinating exhibits such as: the skeleton of the Iguanodon dinosaur and the fossils in the **Sedgwick Museum of Geology**; the skeletons, frogs, bugs, and live pythons in the **Museum of Zoology** (*for both see Route 2, page 25*); and the intriguing relics from Captain Scott's fatal race to reach the South Pole in the **Scott Polar Research Institute** on Lensfield Road (Monday to Friday 9am–5pm, Saturday 9am–1pm). In the **Fitzwilliam Museum** (*see Route 2, pages 27–8*) the favourites with children are the Egyptian mummies and sarcophagi in the Antiquities department, and the armour, swords and fire-arms of the Armoury section. During the summer months the best antidote to sightseeing is the huge but secluded open-air **Jesus Green Swimming Pool**, surrounded by grassy slopes and trees, on Jesus Green, tel: 01223 213352.

Within easy reach of Cambridge, a ride in the simulator capsule at **Duxford Imperial War Museum** (*see page 37*) will delight any would-be pilot. Nature lovers will prefer the **Home Farm** at Wimpole Hall (*see page 37*), where children can mingle with rare breeds of farm animals.

Suffolk and Norfolk have a wide range of attractions for the young, with their beaches, zoos, wildlife centres, waterways, nature reserves and steam railways. Favourite activities include cruising on the **Norfolk Broads** (*see page 71*), taking a ferry trip to **Blakeney Point** to see the seals (*see Tour 5, page 58*), and crabbing along the coast with a basic line and bacon. Boat trips are organised along the estuaries – popular among budding ornithologists.

Wicken Fen near Ely

Blakeney Point for seals

Pleasurewood Hills, Corton Road, Lowestoft, Suffolk (tel: 01502 508200) is one of the largest **theme parks** in the country and the Pleasure Beach leisure centre at Great Yarmouth offers six acres of rides and attractions. Daily entertainment, in the form of giant mechanical organs and the Wurlitzer show, is offered at the **Thursford Collection** at Thursford, Norfolk (Easter to October, daily 12.30–5.30pm). For young children the **Dinosaur Natural History Park**, Weston Estate, Weston Longville, Norfolk (March to October, daily 10am–5pm) has life-size models of dinosaurs along trails through unspoilt woodland. Appealing to all ages is the **Otter Trust** at Earsham, Bungay, Norfolk (Easter to October daily, 10.30am–6pm) which has the world's largest collection of otters amid beautiful surroundings on the banks of the River Waveney. In Essex, **Colchester Castle** (*see Tour 2, page 44*) is very much geared to children, with its hands-on exhibits, audio presentations and costumes to try on.

Accommodation

B&Bs are plentiful

Cambridge has a limited number of hotels, particularly noticeable in the busy months of June and July. Outstanding hotels are hard to come by, and there are very few small hotels within the city of any real charm or character. The Tourist Information Centre (*see page 75*) has information on accommodation and will reserve rooms for a small fee plus 10 percent of the cost of the stay. Guest Houses and Bed and Breakfasts are plentiful, many of them located on the edge of the city. Suffolk and Norfolk have a number of delightful rural hotels, some of them converted from manor houses, farms or coaching inns.

Cambridge

££££ (over £150 per night double)
Garden House Hotel, Granta Place, Mill Lane, tel: 01223 259988, fax: 316605. The most desirable hotel in Cambridge, thanks to its splendid riverside setting close to the city centre. Modern lounge, bar and conservatory make the most of the location, and there are punts in the neighbouring boatyard for trips to Grantchester or the Backs. 118 bedrooms. Restaurant, coffee shop, gift shop.

University Arms Hotel

Arundel House Hotel

£££ (over £100 per night double)
Holiday Inn, Downing Street, tel: 01223 464466, fax: 464440. Large, modern hotel with an incongruous neo-classical facade, built, amid much controversy, in the heart of the city. Open-plan public areas, courtyard garden, restaurant, 199 comfortable bedrooms. Latest changes involve the conversion of the swimming pool into conference facilities. **University Arms Hotel**, Regent Street, tel: 01223 351241, fax: 461319. Fine location overlooking Parker's Piece, and close to the city centre. Victorian building, where traditions have been maintained. The wood-panelled dining room overlooks the green.

££ (over £60 per night double)
Arundel House Hotel, 53 Chesterton Road, tel: 01223 367701, fax: 367721. Elegantly furnished hotel, converted from three Victorian houses. 10 minutes' walk from the centre, with the River Cam across the road. Restaurant. **Cambridge Lodge Hotel**, 139 Huntingdon Road, tel: 01223 352833. Small hotel in an upmarket residential area 1½ miles (2.5km) from the city centre. Popular restaurant.

£ (under £60 per night double)
De Freville House, 166 Chesterton Road, tel: 01223 354993, fax 321890. Family-run, Victorian house on quiet, residential street close to the River Cam and a short walk from the city centre. Non-smokers only. **Purlins**, 12 High

Street, Little Shelford, Cambridge, tel/fax: 01223 842643. Attractively furnished guest house with two acres of woodland and lawns in conservation area of quiet village, 4 miles (6.5km) south of Cambridge. Pubs and restaurants nearby. **The Suffolk House**, 69 Milton Road, tel: 01223 352016, fax: 566816. Small family-run guest house with own garden and parking. 20 minutes walk from centre.

Country
Suffolk

Angel Hotel, Angel Hill, Bury St Edmunds, tel: 01284 753926, fax 750092. Overlooking the Abbey gardens, this has been an inn since 1452. Friendly, with plenty of character. Front rooms can be noisy. ££. **Black Lion**, The Green, Long Melford, tel: 01787 312356, fax: 374557. Restored 17th-century coaching inn on the green with attractive lounge and bedrooms. Children very welcome. ££. **Old Rectory**, Campsea Ashe, tel: 01728 746524. Georgian country house and gardens in a quiet village close to Woodbridge. Highly recommended for food. Nine bedrooms only. ££. **The Crown**, 90 High Street, Southwold, tel: 01502 722275, fax: 724805. 18th-century inn owned by Adnams wine merchants. Emphasis on the restaurant, serving excellent cuisine and wines. 12 bedrooms only, mostly with en-suite facilities. ££

Angel Hotel

Norfolk

Cley Mill, Cley-Next-The-Sea, tel/fax: 01263 740209. Renovated 18th-century mill overlooking the marshes. Friendly, private-home atmosphere. Restaurant, with good food. Self-catering apartments available. ££

Essex

Hintlesham Hall, Hintlesham, nr Ipswich, tel: 01473 652268, fax: 652463. 16th-century mansion, but now essentially Georgian. Highly civilised with elegant decor throughout. Friendly atmosphere, excellent food. 33 luxurious rooms, garden, tennis, golf, outdoor swimming pool, gym and sauna. £££. **Maison Talbooth**, Stratford Road, Dedham, near Colchester, tel: 01206 322367, fax: 322752. The most luxurious B&B in East Anglia. Victorian house with 10 lavishly furnished rooms. Guests can eat at Le Talbooth under the same management, a quarter of a mile away (*see page 68*). ££££. **Old House**, Fordstreet, Aldham, Nr Colchester, tel: 01206 240456. 14th-century, Grade II listed building. Friendly family home with exposed beams, log fires, large garden and pond. No restaurant but three pubs with food close by. £ **The Angel**, Market Place, Lavenham, tel: 01787 247388. Medieval inn overlooking the market place. Also recommended for food. ££

Maison Talbooth

Lavenham

Index